PRAISE FOR

THE BOOK OF JOE

"Wake up and smell the coffee! Daniel Misdea's *The Book of Joe* is an exciting debut from a fresh and funny voice. This charming book is the transformative tale of how even a weak cup of coffee can become strong."

—PATRICK MCDONNELL (*Mutts*, Cartoonist)

"Daniel Misdea's *The Book of Joe* made me laugh, and feel sympathetic towards a cup of coffee. Now I can't go to Starbucks without chuckling or getting emotional."

—LONNIE MILLSAP (*bacön*, Cartoonist)

"If a sentient cup of coffee can find friendship, there's hope for all of us!"

—ELIZABETH PICH (*Fun Girl*, Cartoonist)

"Dan is a wildly creative, funny & prolific comic. I loved this insightful & witty story of a journey that reflects what it means to be human. I developed compassion for Joe as he faced the heartaches and rock bottoms that ultimately catalyze one to search for meaning and purpose. *The Book of Joe* is well written, well sequenced, and well received!"

—LOU REDMOND (*Find Your Truth*, Author)

"It's always refreshing to see the work of a new cartoonist as they carve out their niche in the world of scribbling, even more so when they are as witty and talented as Daniel Misdea. *The Book of Joe* is a fun and insightful read"

—MARK LYNCH (Cartoonist)

"I'm a big fan of coffee and few books capture the spirit of coffee quite like *The Book of Joe*. Both touching and delightful, *The Book of Joe* is sure to make you think twice before treating a cup of coffee thoughtlessly ever, ever again. If it doesn't, then you don't have a soul."

—BRAD PERRI (*Pirate Mike*, Cartoonist)

THE BOOK OF JOE

By: Daniel Misdea

THE BOOK OF JOE

by Daniel Misdea

ISBN 978-1-63393-784-0

More about *The Book of Joe* and Daniel Misdea at:
boldcoarseblend@gmail.com
www.boldcoarseblend.com
instagram: @bcb_comics
twitter: @bcb_comics

Published by

210 60th Street
Virginia Beach, VA 23451
800-435-4811
www.koehlerbooks.com

"I AM WRITING THIS NOT FOR THE EYES OF
THE MANY, BUT FOR YOURS ALONE:
FOR EACH OF US IS AUDIENCE
ENOUGH FOR THE OTHER."

-EPICURUS

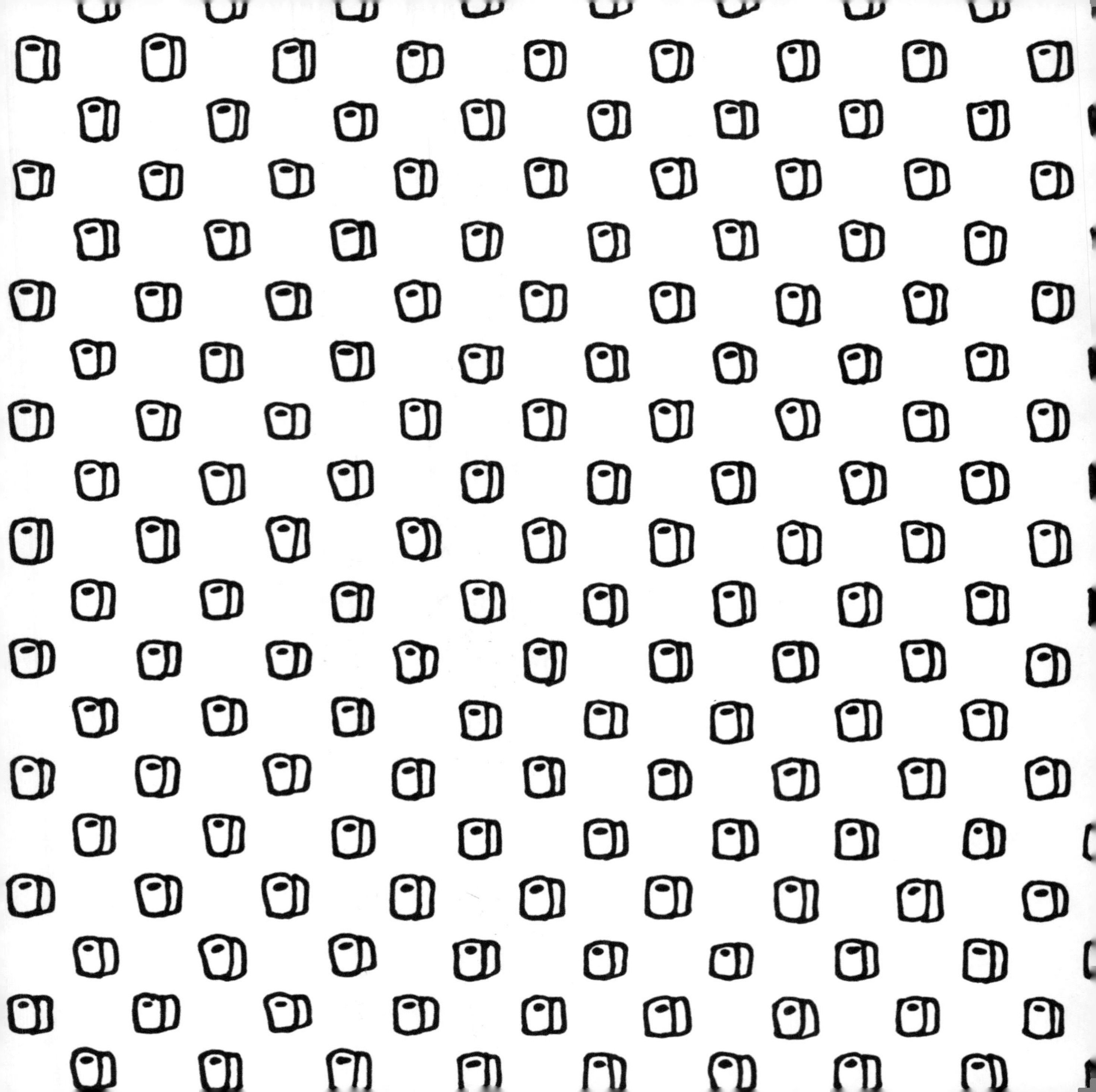

JOE LOVED HIS LATTE

HE LOVED HER SO MUCH

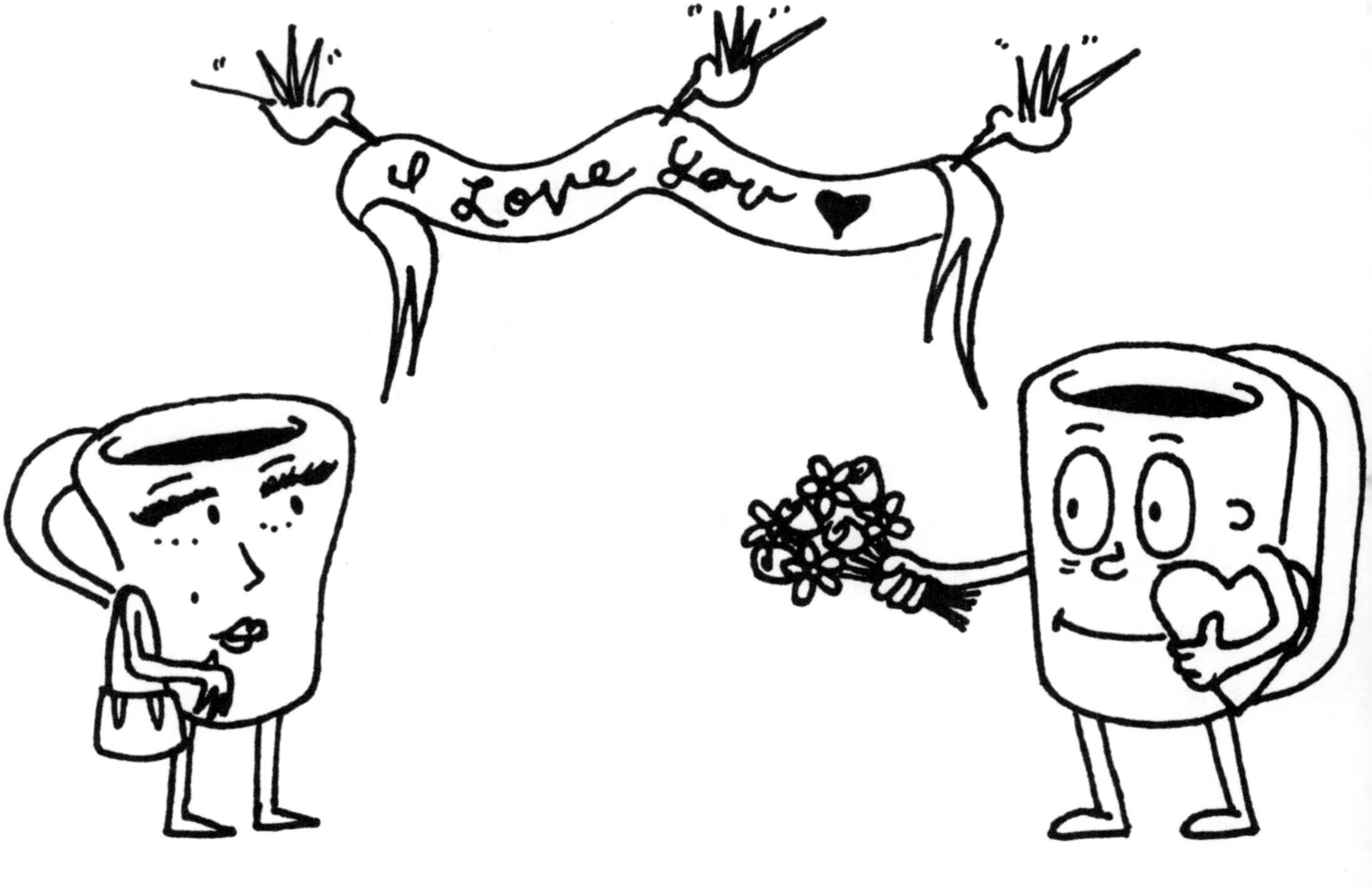
I Love You

HE TOOK HER TO BREAKFAST
AND HE TOOK HER TO BRUNCH

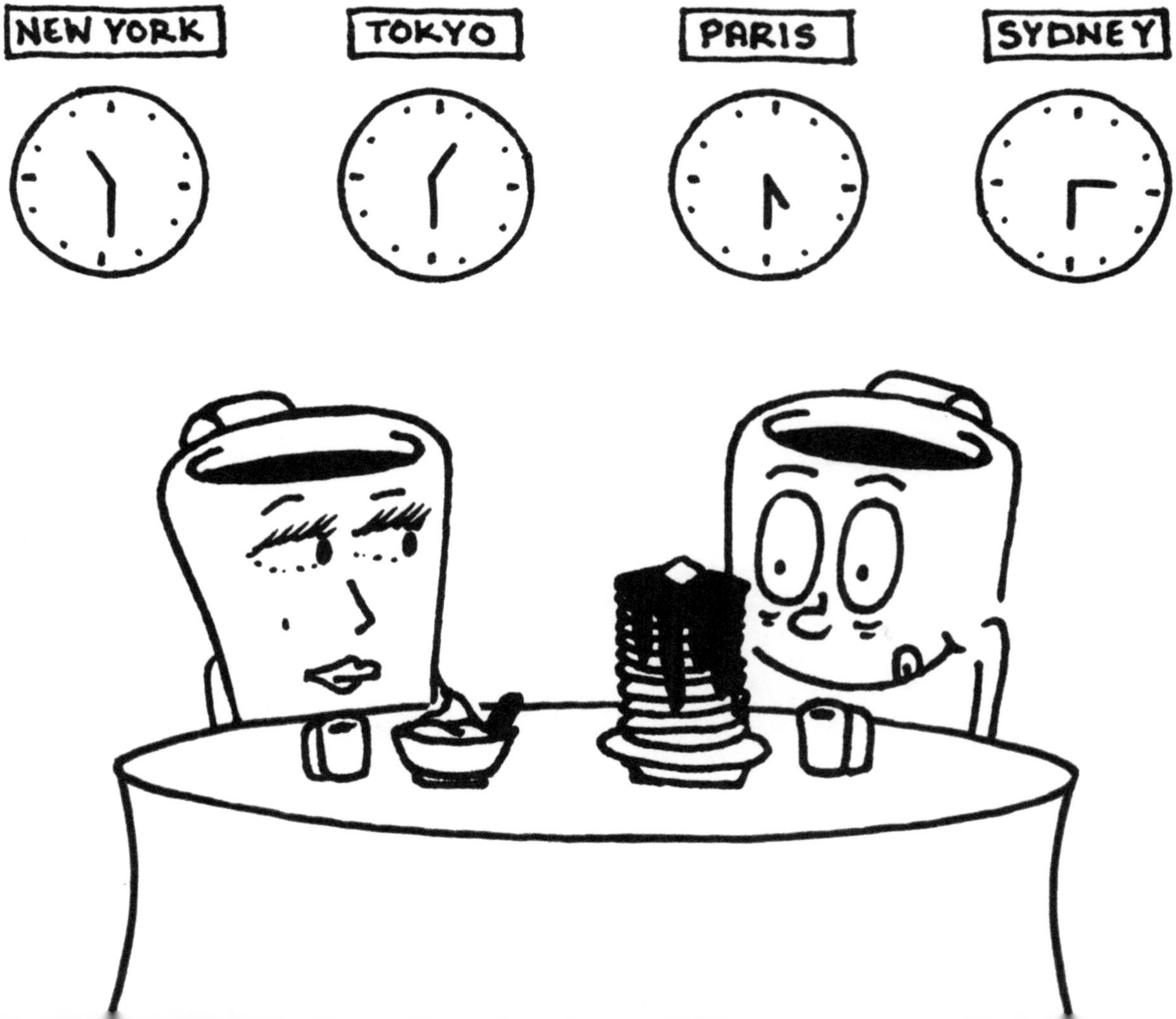
NEW YORK
TOKYO
PARIS
SYDNEY

BUT THEN SHE LEFT HIM...

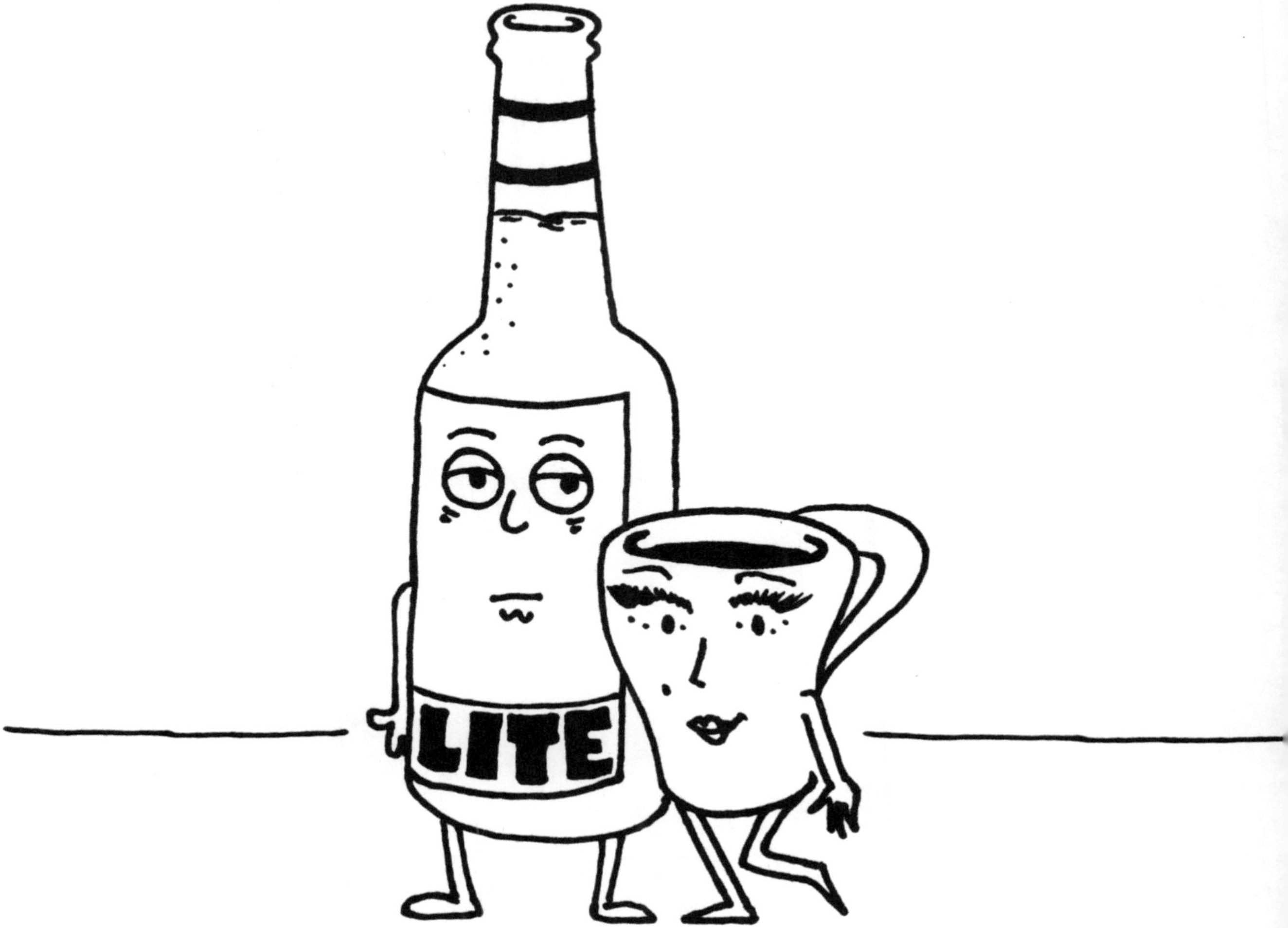
LITE

FOR A BOTTLE OF BEER

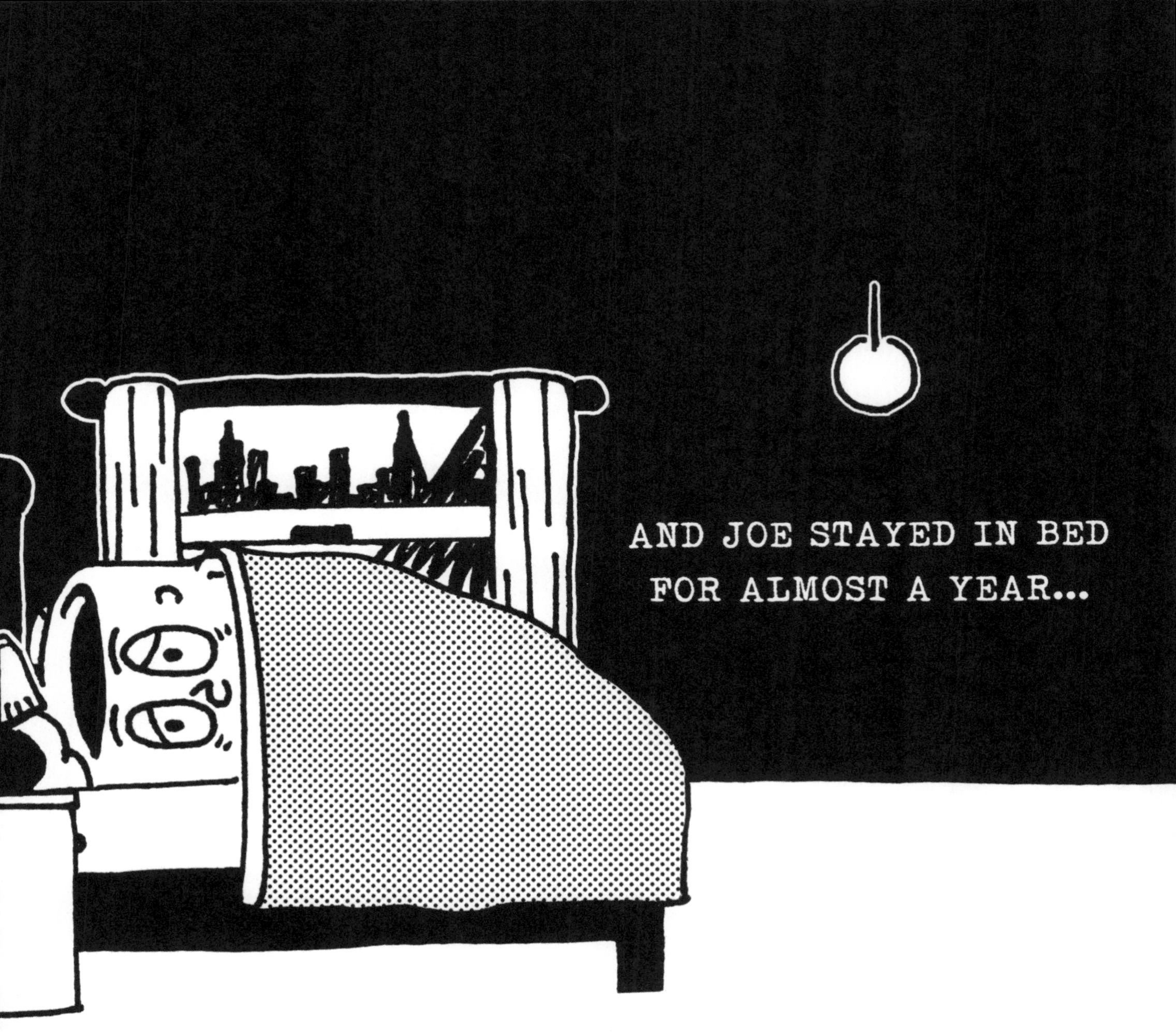
AND JOE STAYED IN BED
FOR ALMOST A YEAR...

JOE'S CONFIDENCE SHRANK
SO HE SMOKED AND HE DRANK

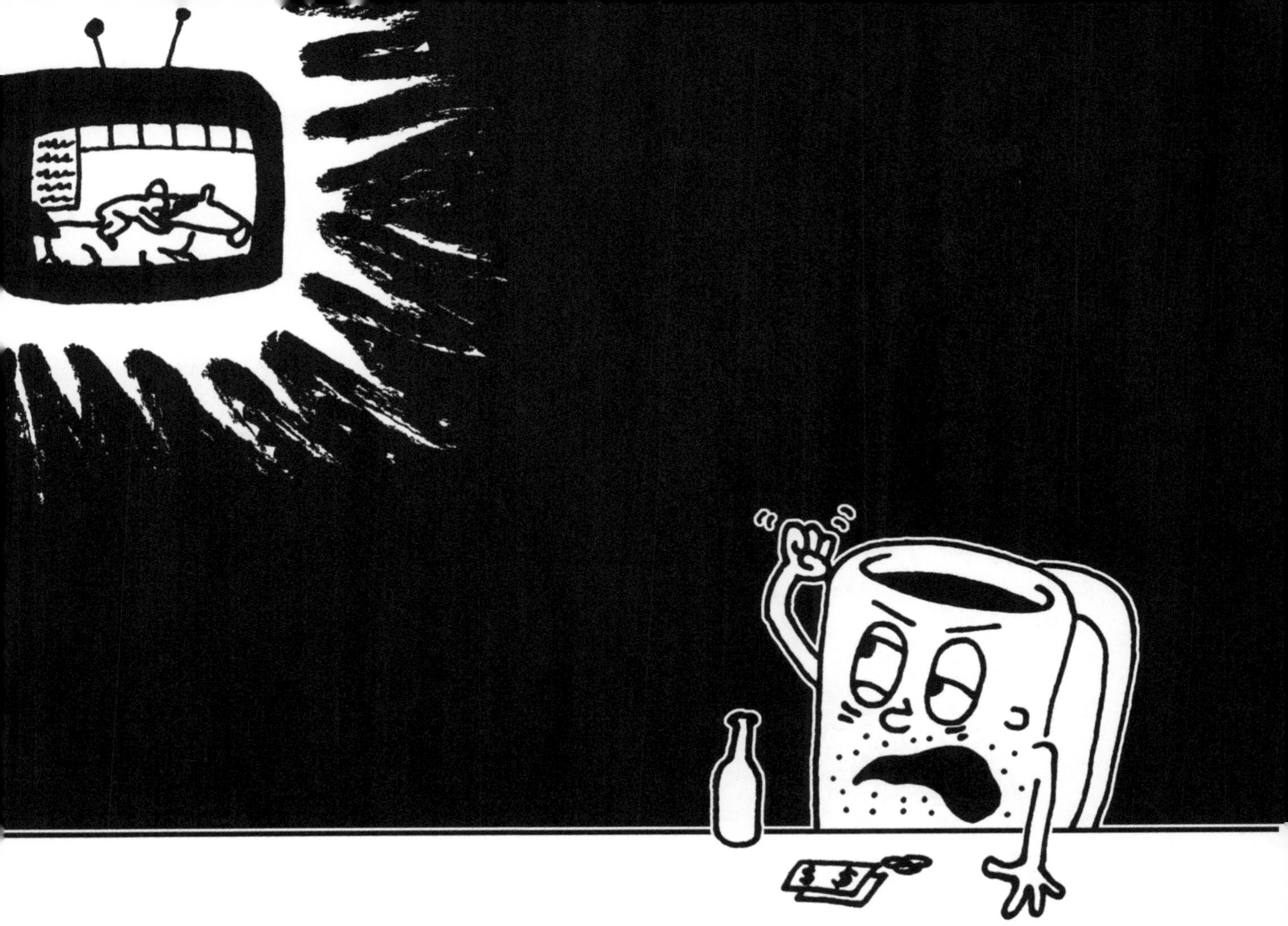

AND HE LOST ALL THE MONEY
THAT HE PUT IN THE BANK

THEN A LADY IN RED

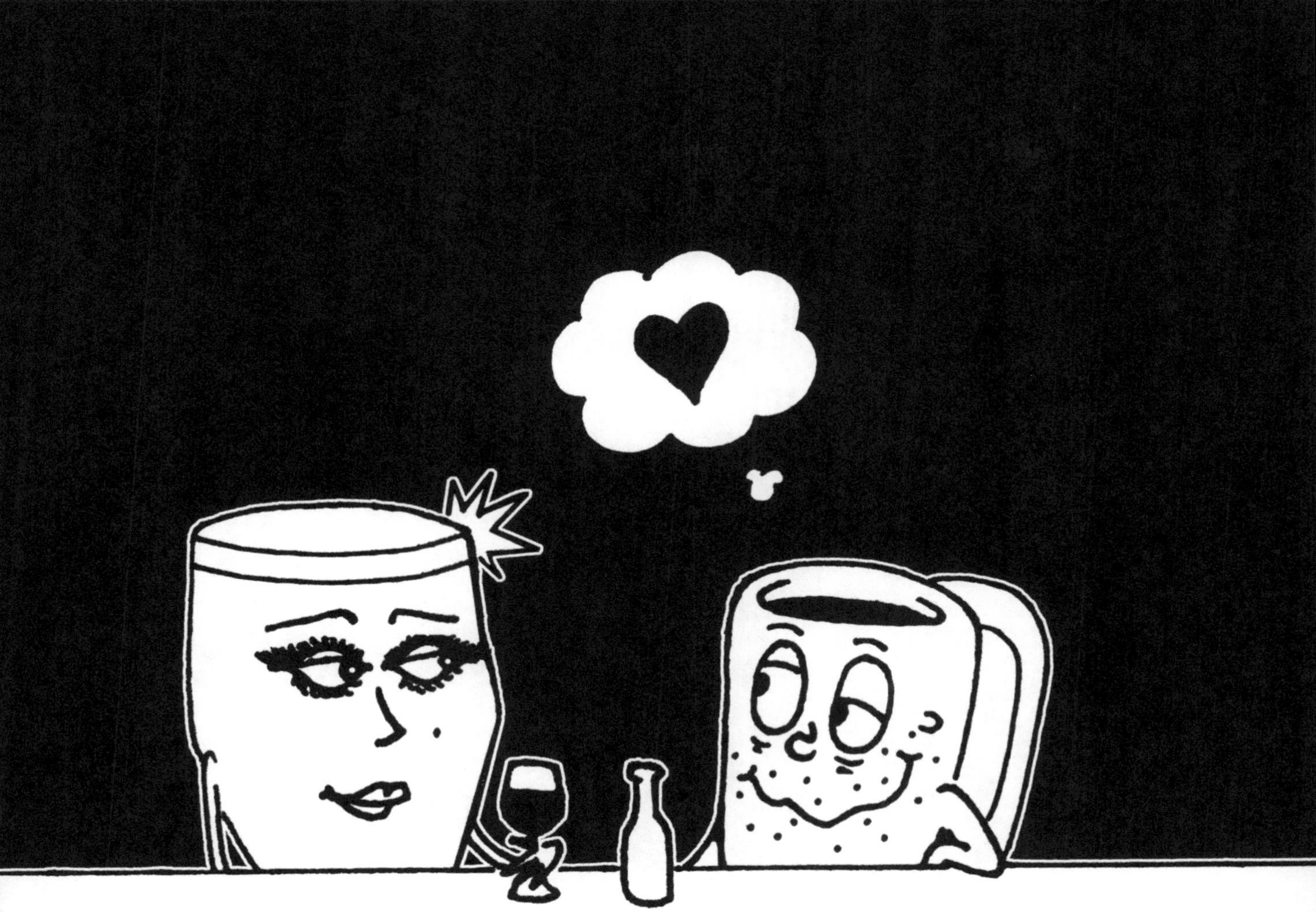

SENT A CHILL UP HIS SPINE

AND JOE FELL IN LOVE
WITH A TALL GLASS OF WINE...

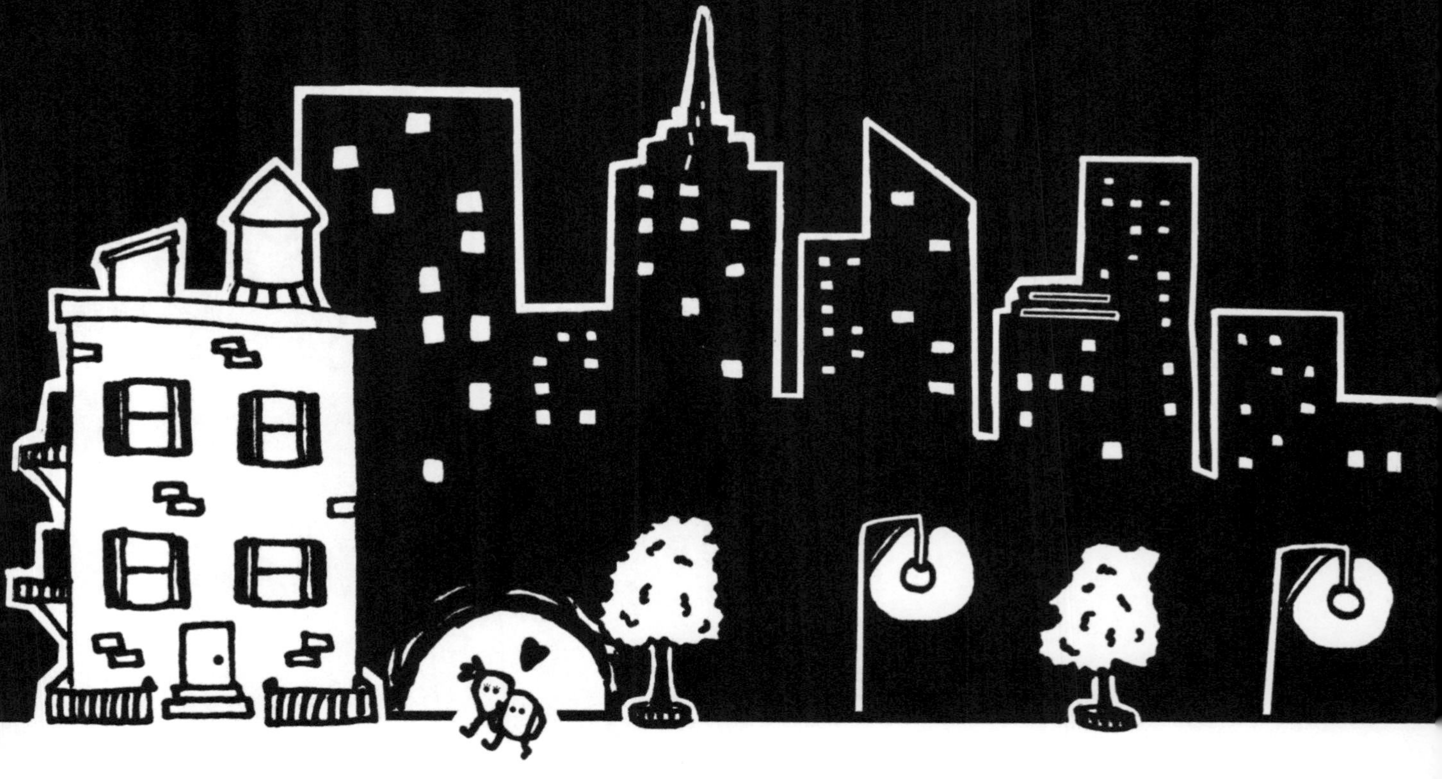

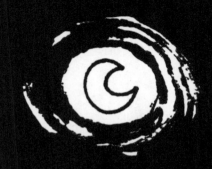

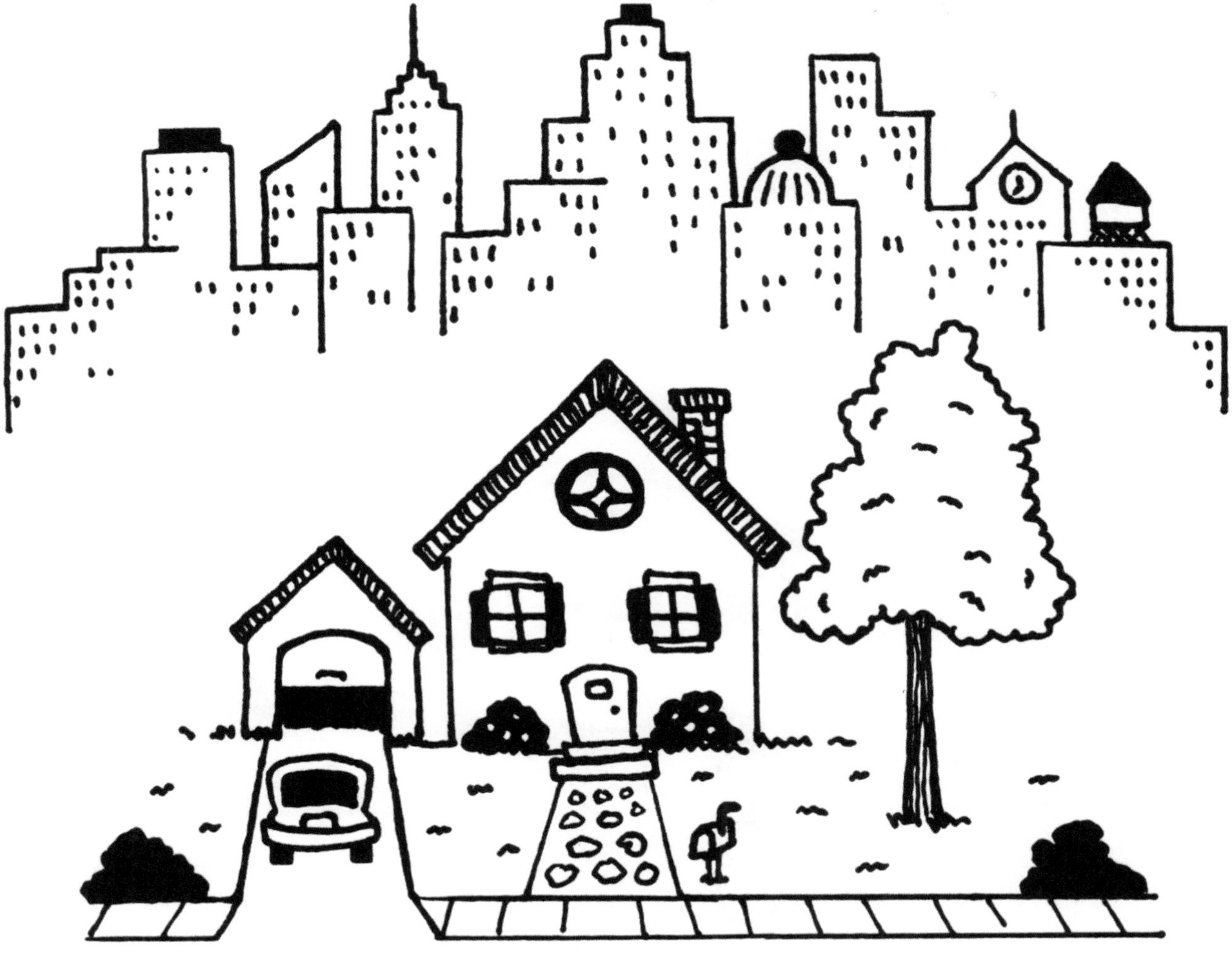

THEY BOUGHT A SMALL HOUSE

ONE DAY JOE CAME HOME

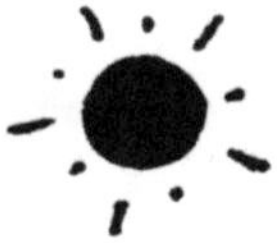

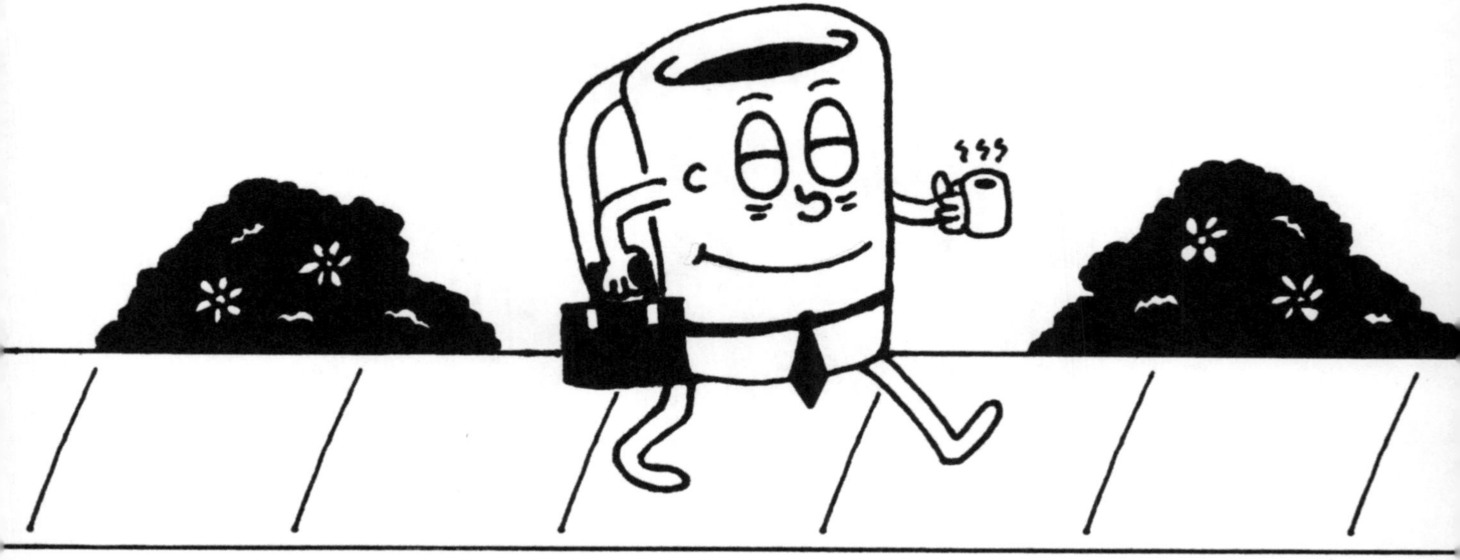

TO THINK
THAT HE'D FIND

HIS FINE WINE ALONE

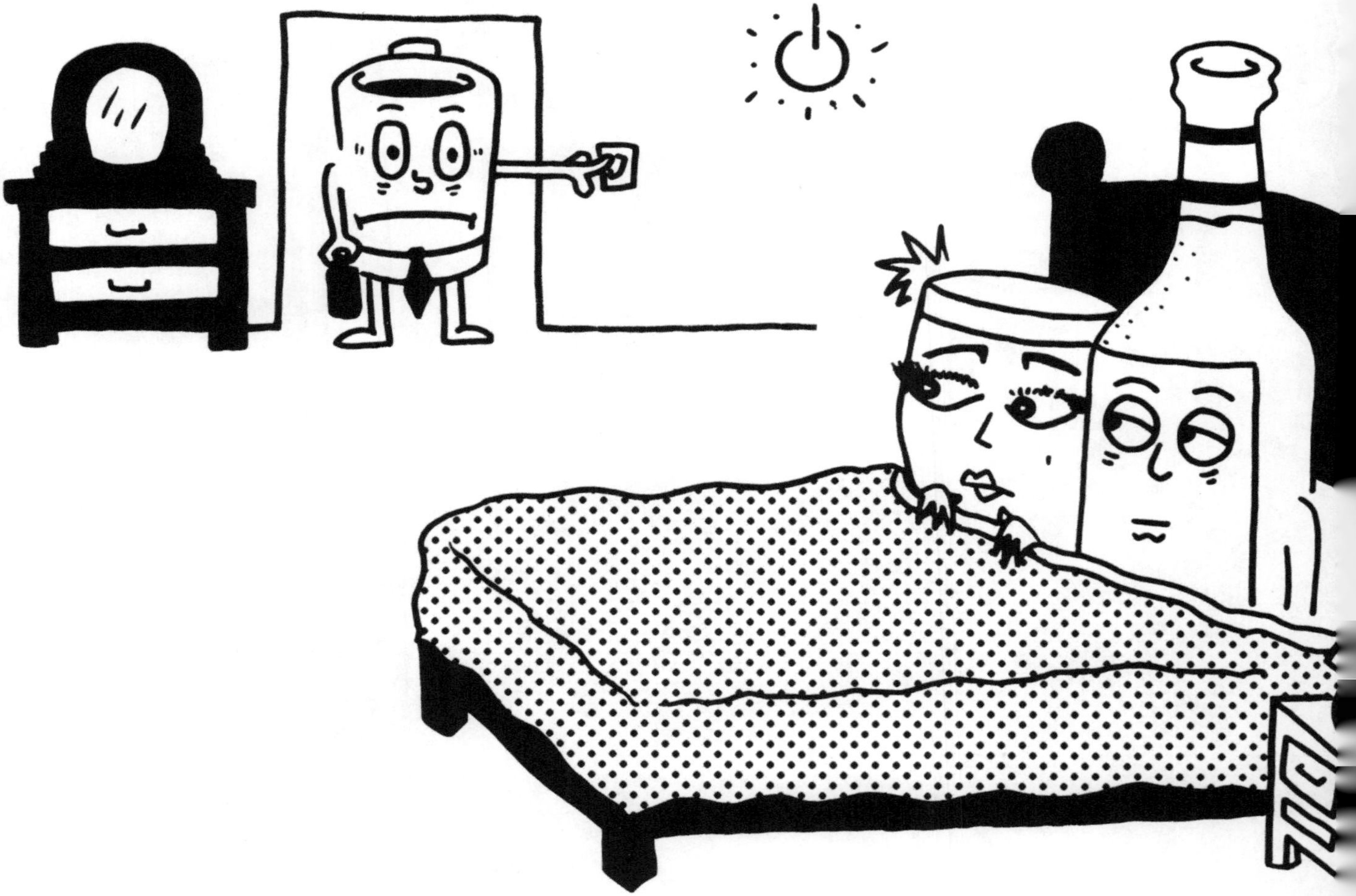

SO HE FLED TO THE CITY

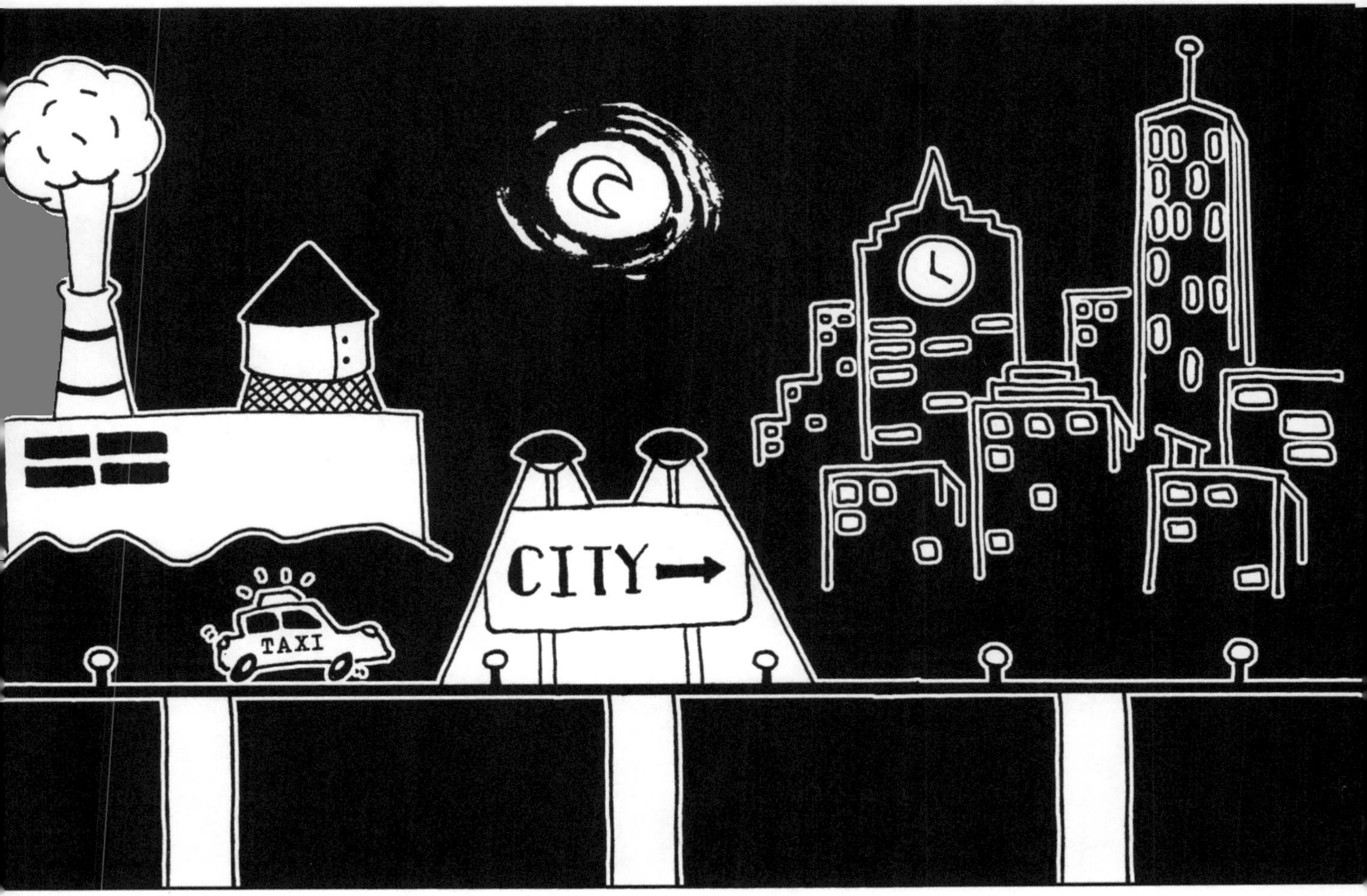
TAXI
CITY→

TO DROWN IN HIS SHAME

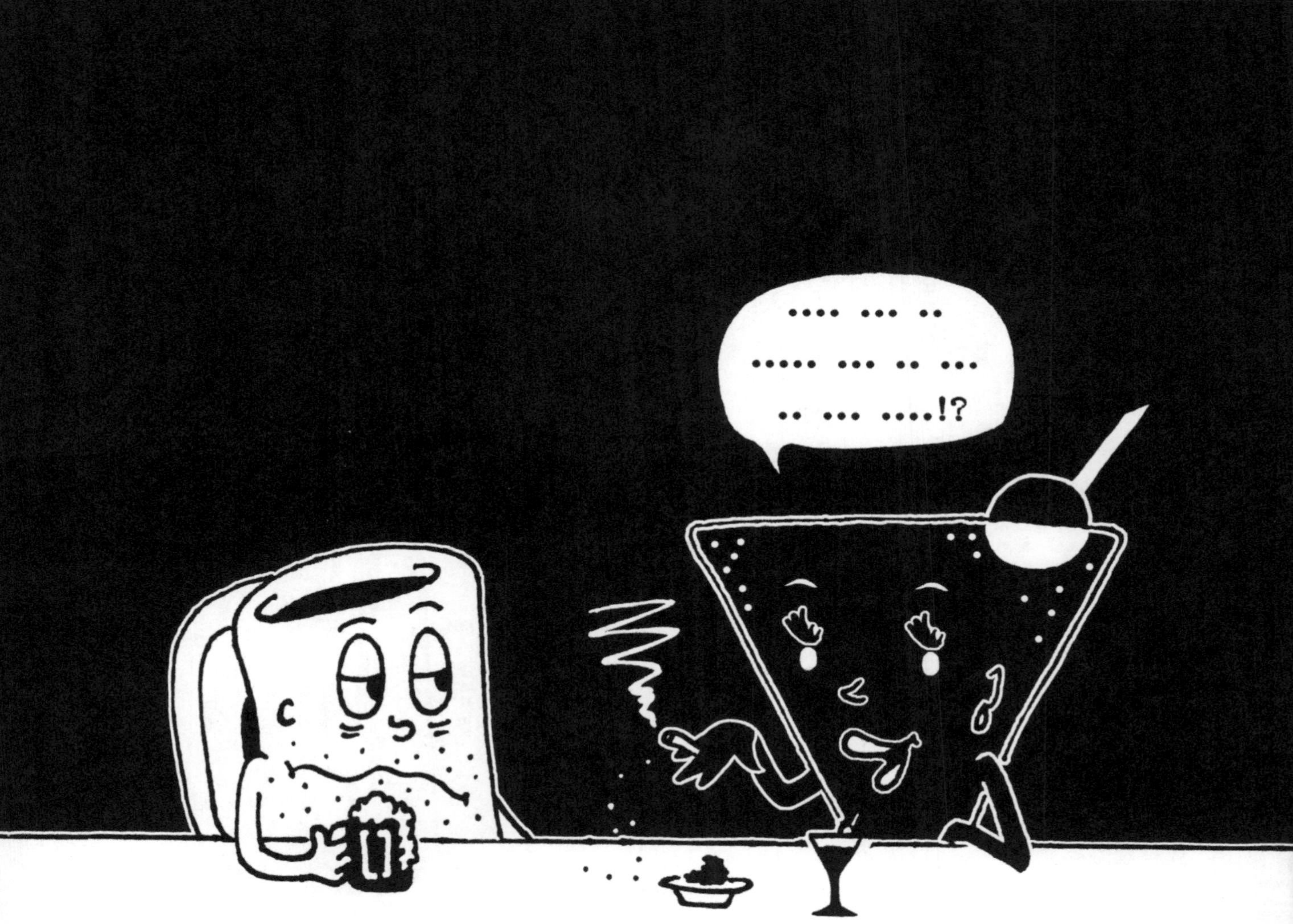
....!?

HE MET A MARTINI

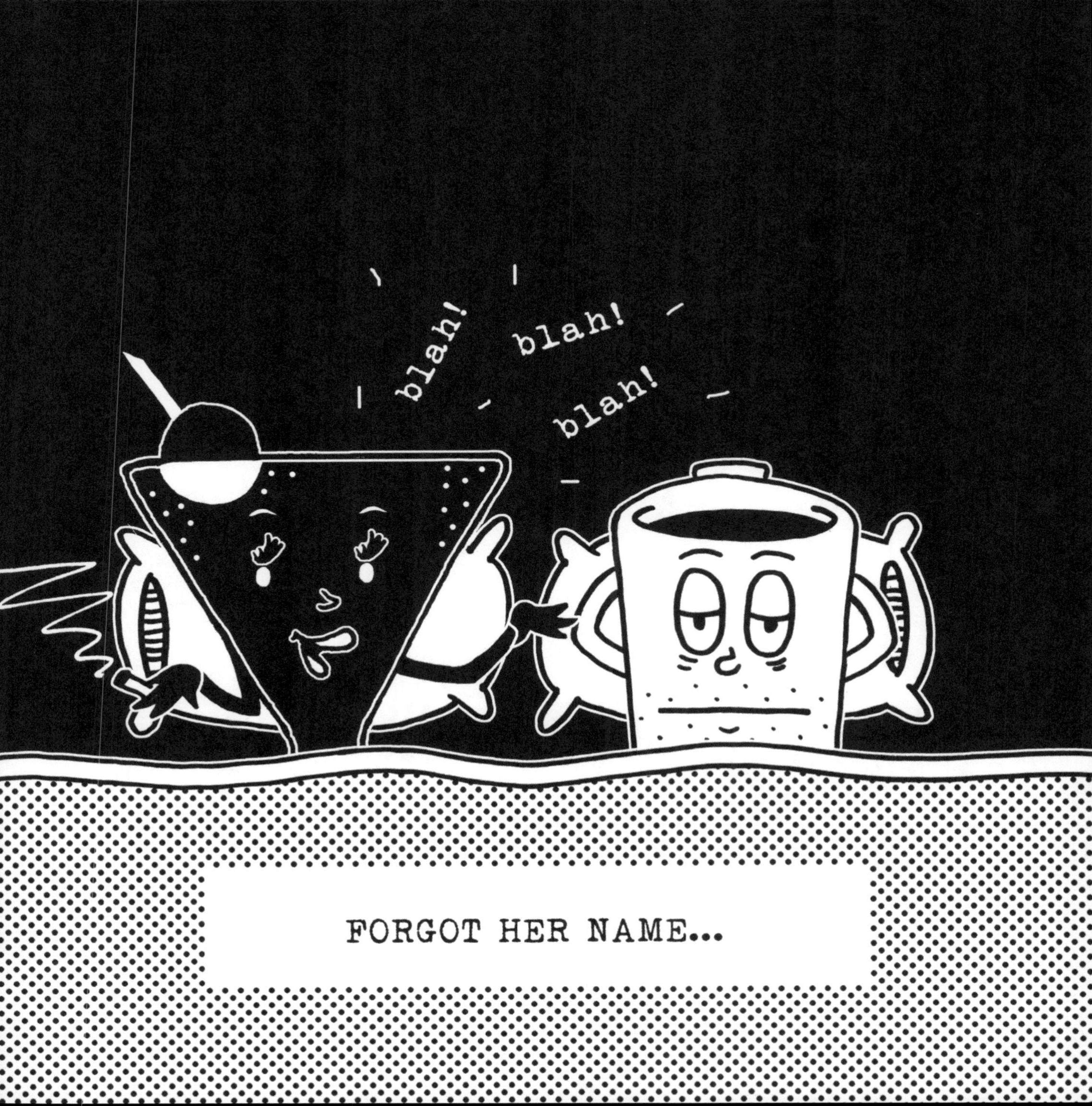
blah!
blah!
blah!
FORGOT HER NAME...

HE TRIED
PAINTING

AND JOGGING

HE TRIED MEDITATION

HE TRIED
LIFTING WEIGHTS

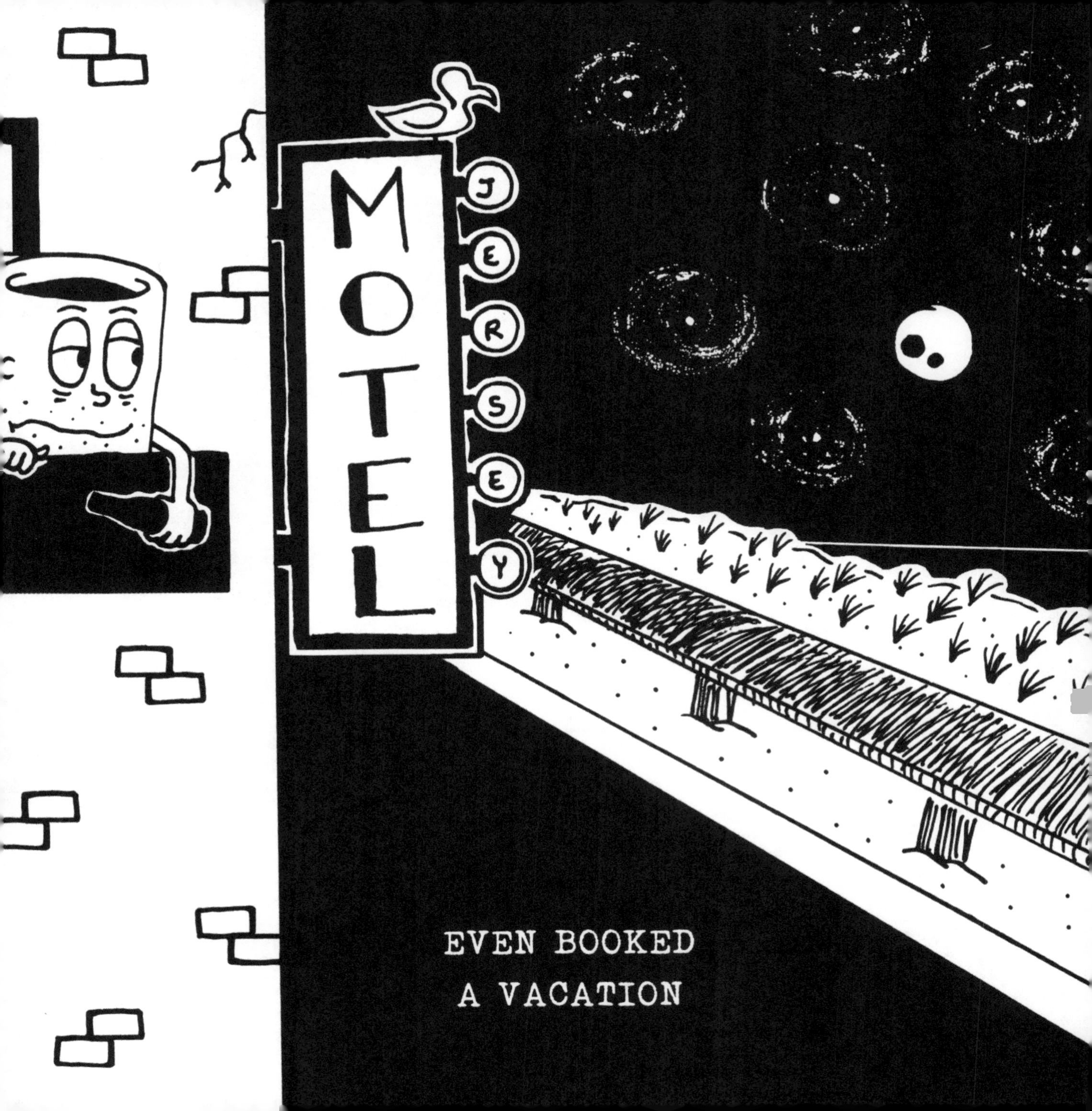
MOTEL
JERSEY
EVEN BOOKED
A VACATION

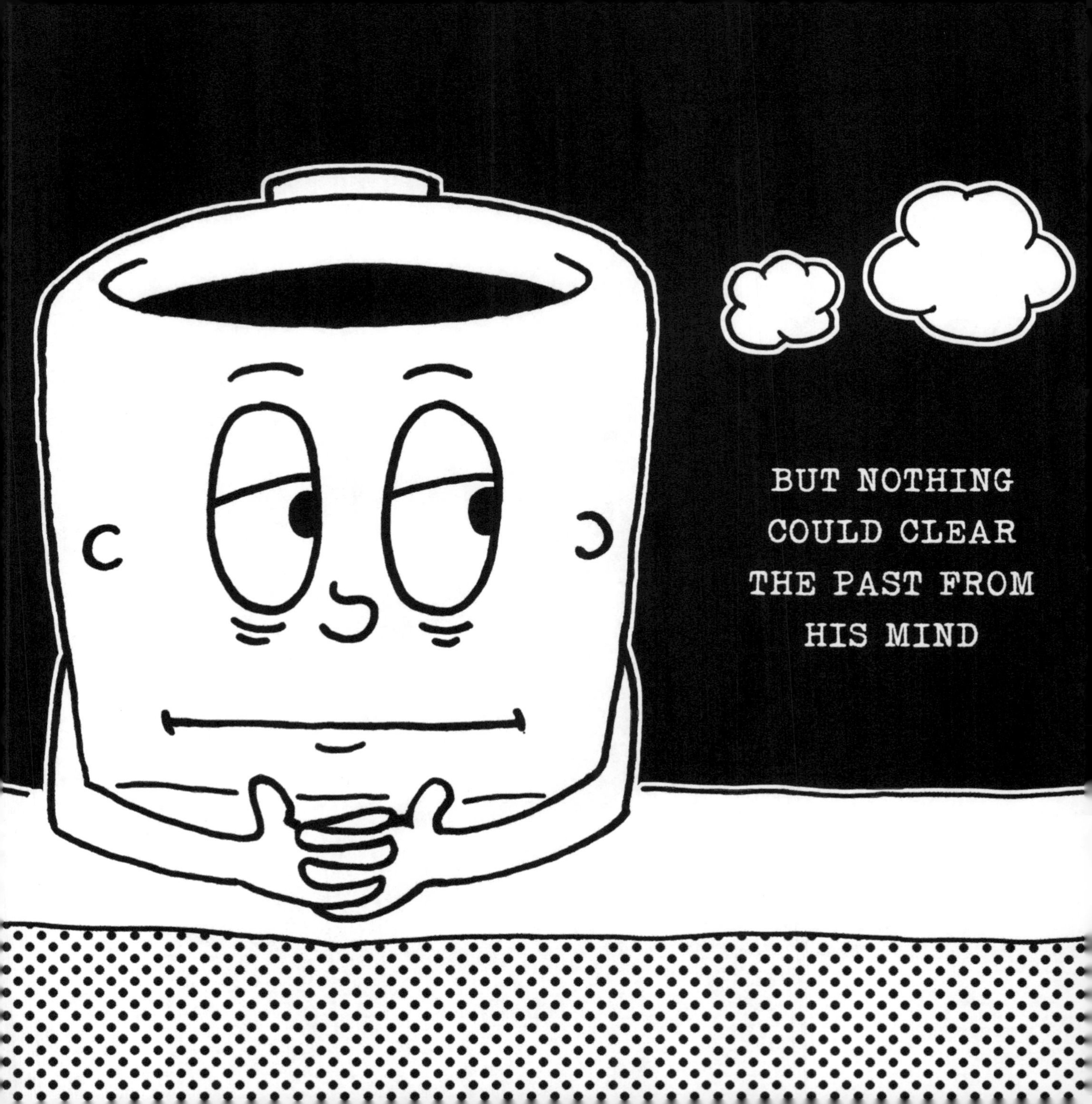
BUT NOTHING COULD CLEAR THE PAST FROM HIS MIND

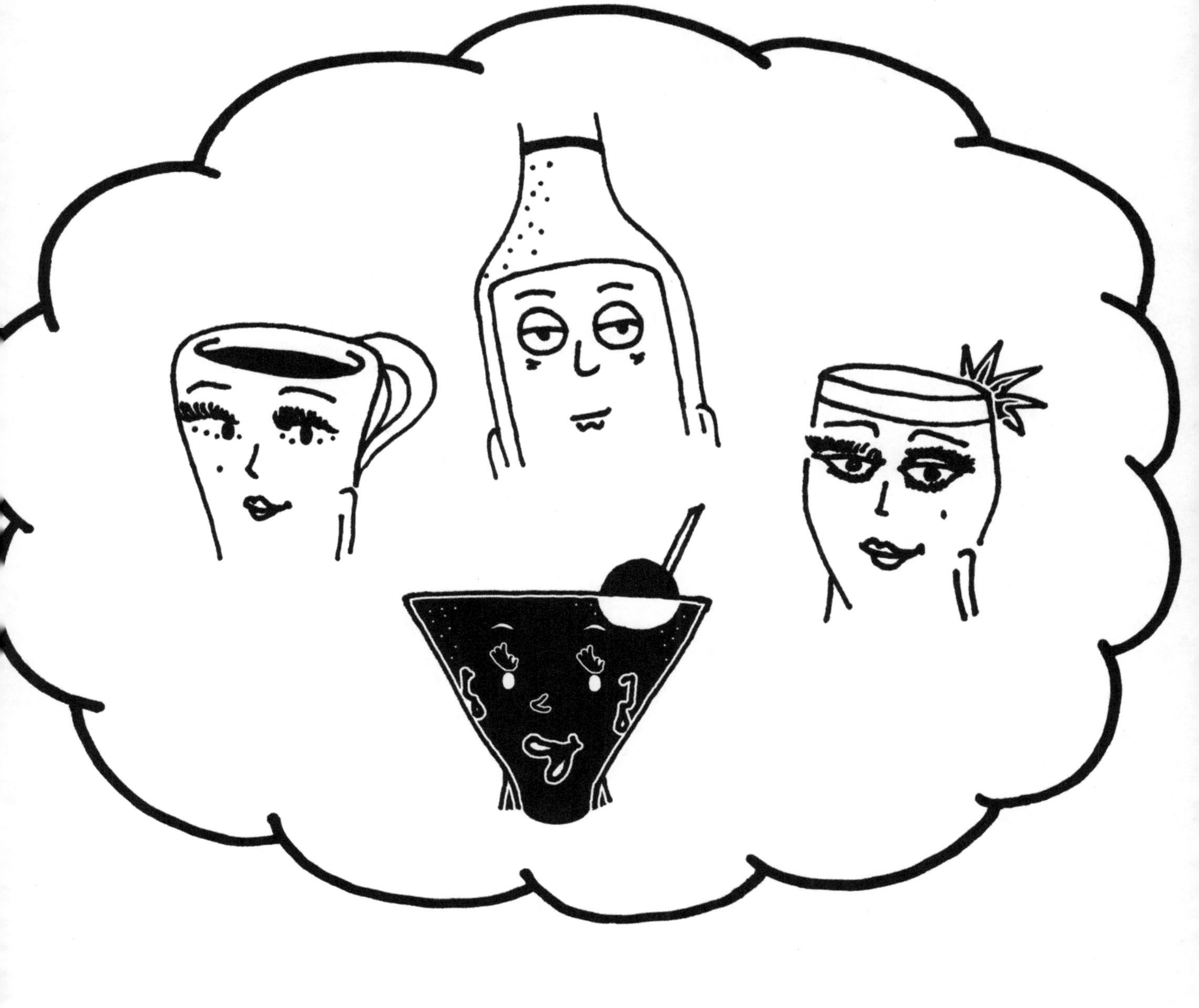

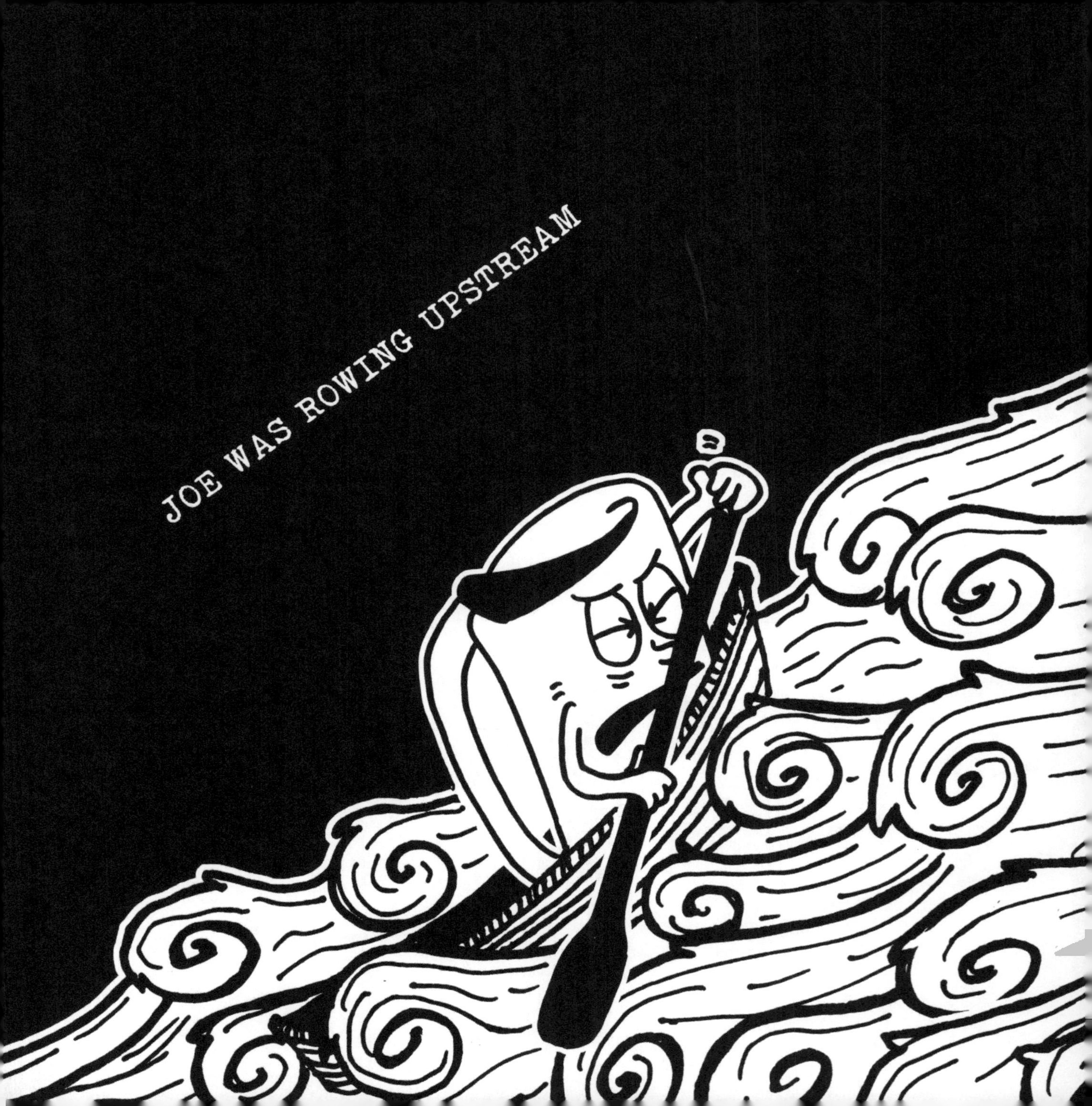
JOE WAS ROWING UPSTREAM

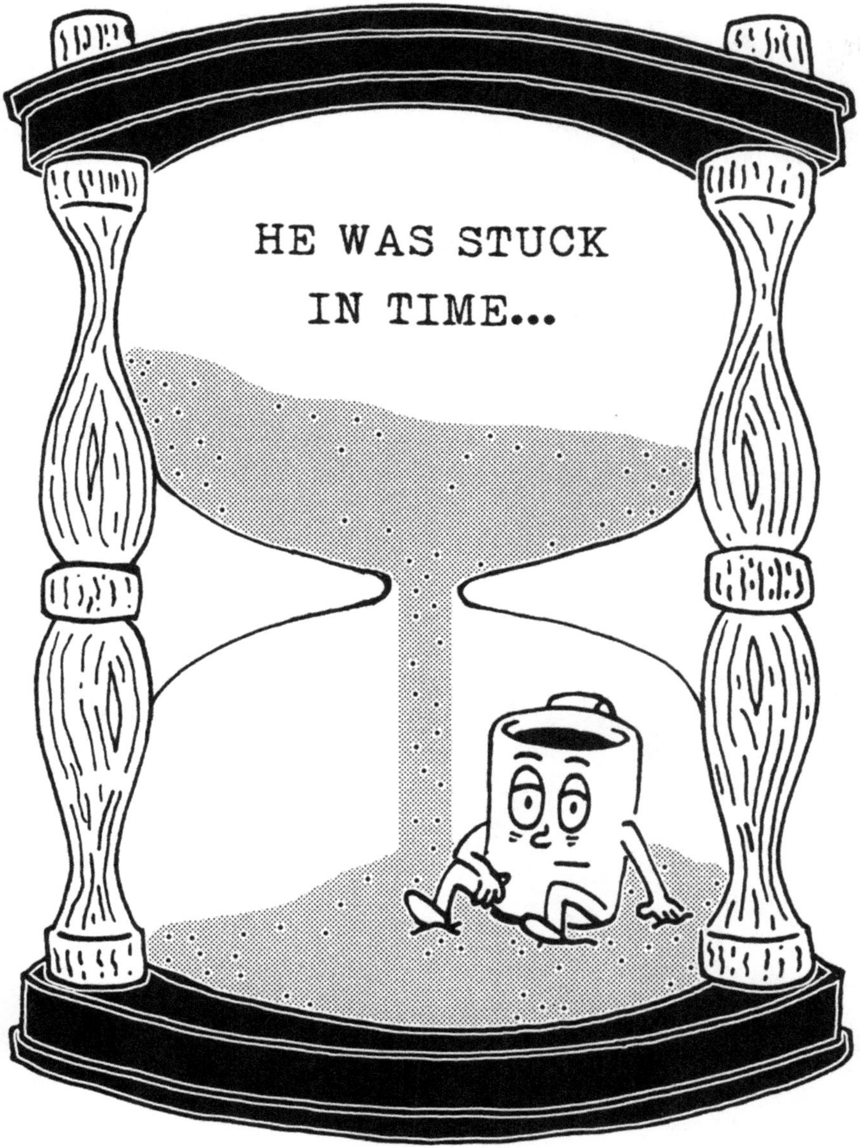
HE WAS STUCK
IN TIME...

SO HE STAYED UP
ALL NIGHT
AND LAID ON
THE GROUND

UNTIL ONE DAY
HE WENT TO THE
PET STORE
IN TOWN

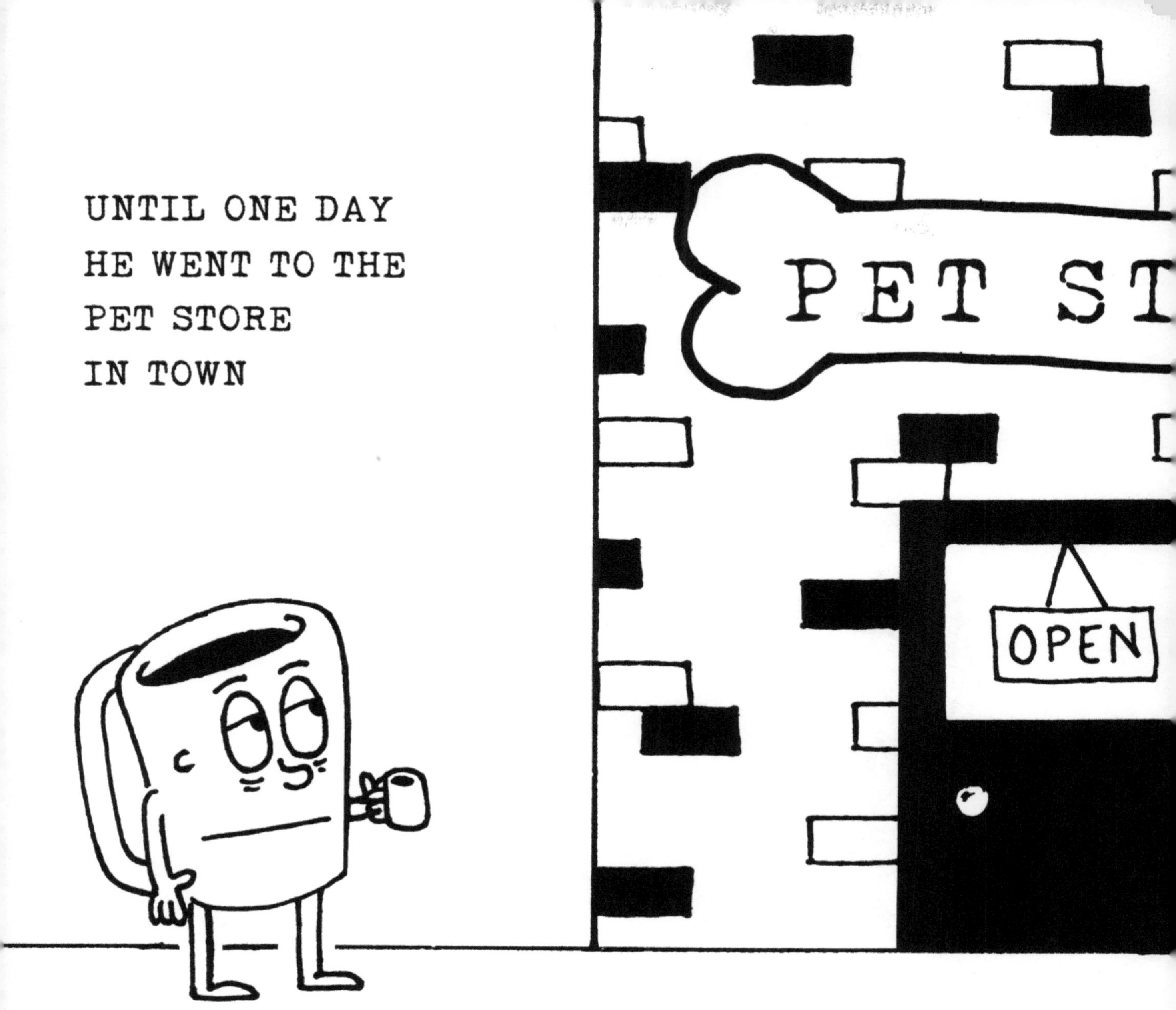
PET ST
OPEN

WHERE HE WAS CHASED BY A DOG

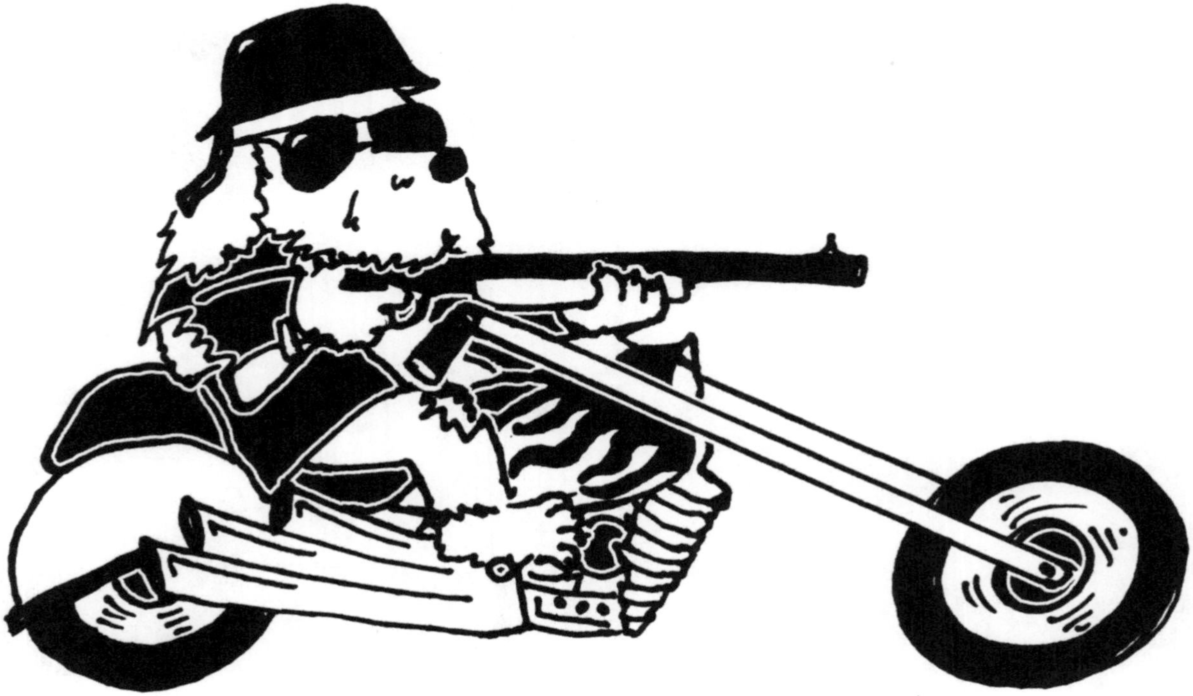

STUNG BY A BEE

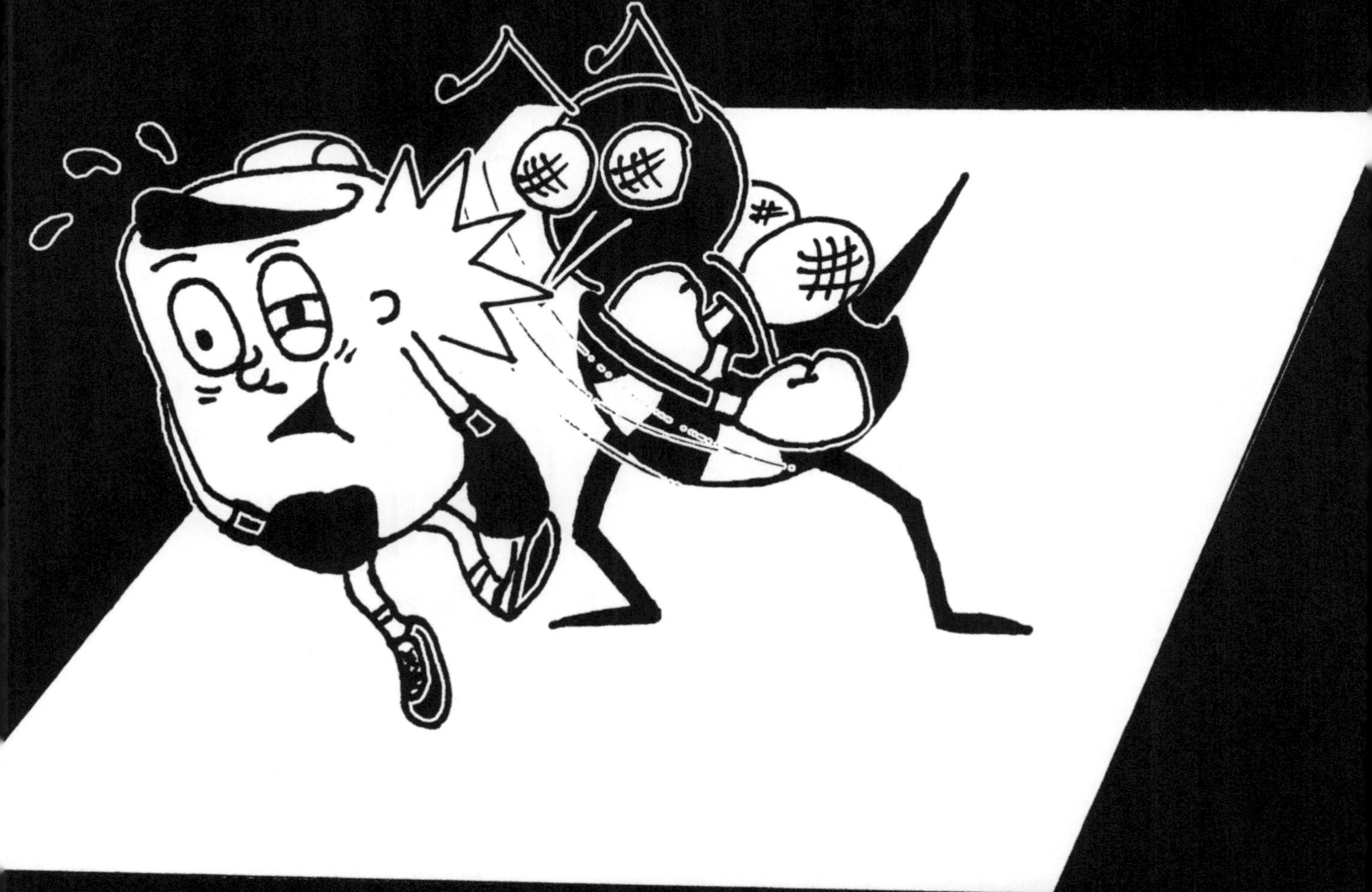

BIT BY A SNAKE

AND MET OSCAR
THE MONKEY...

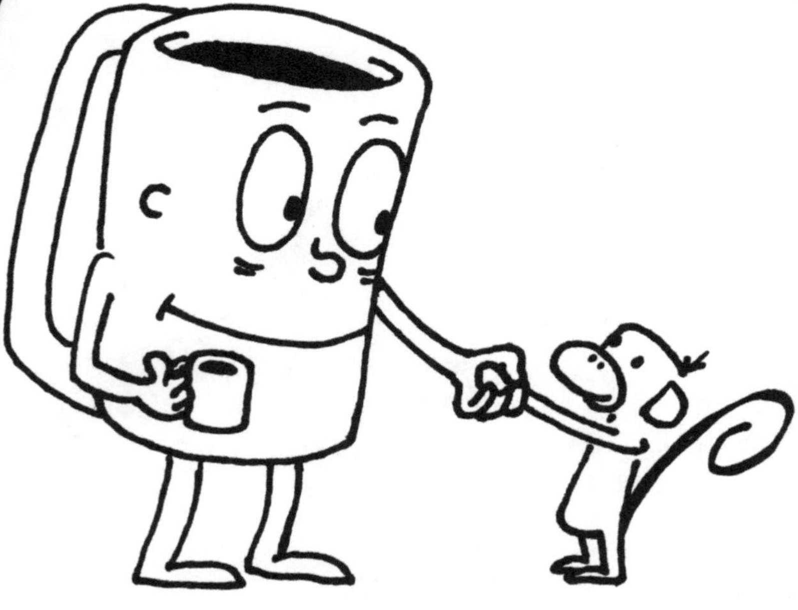

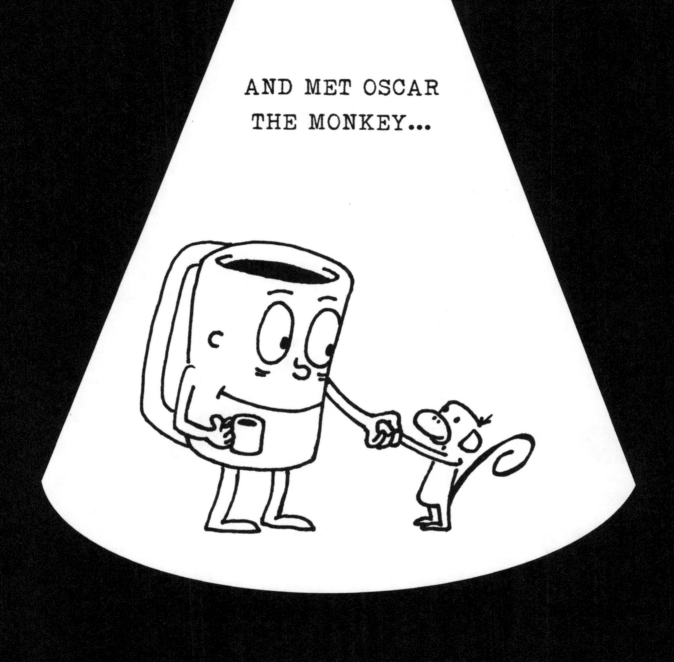

THEY PLAYED CATCH
IN A CORNFIELD

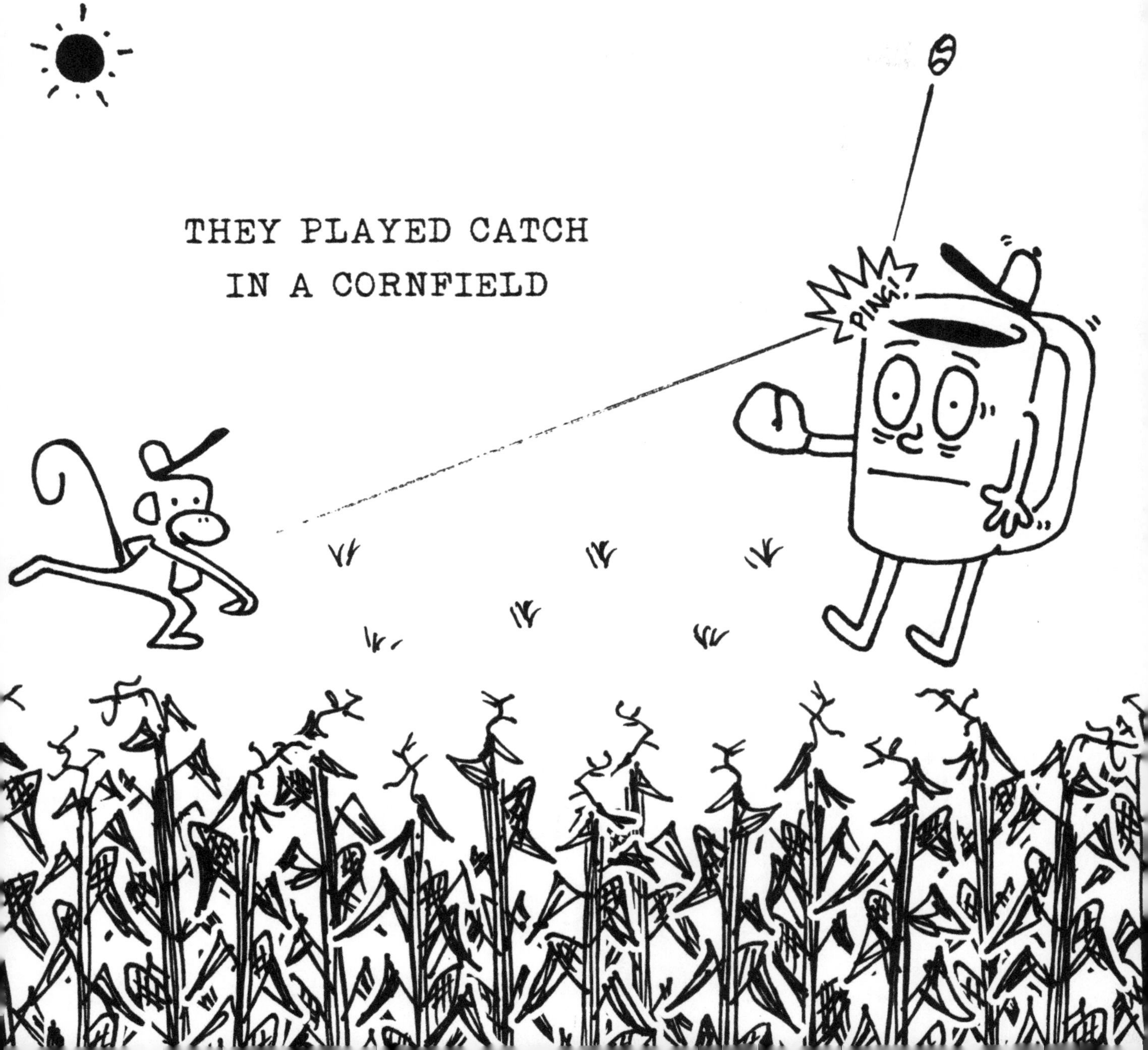
PING!

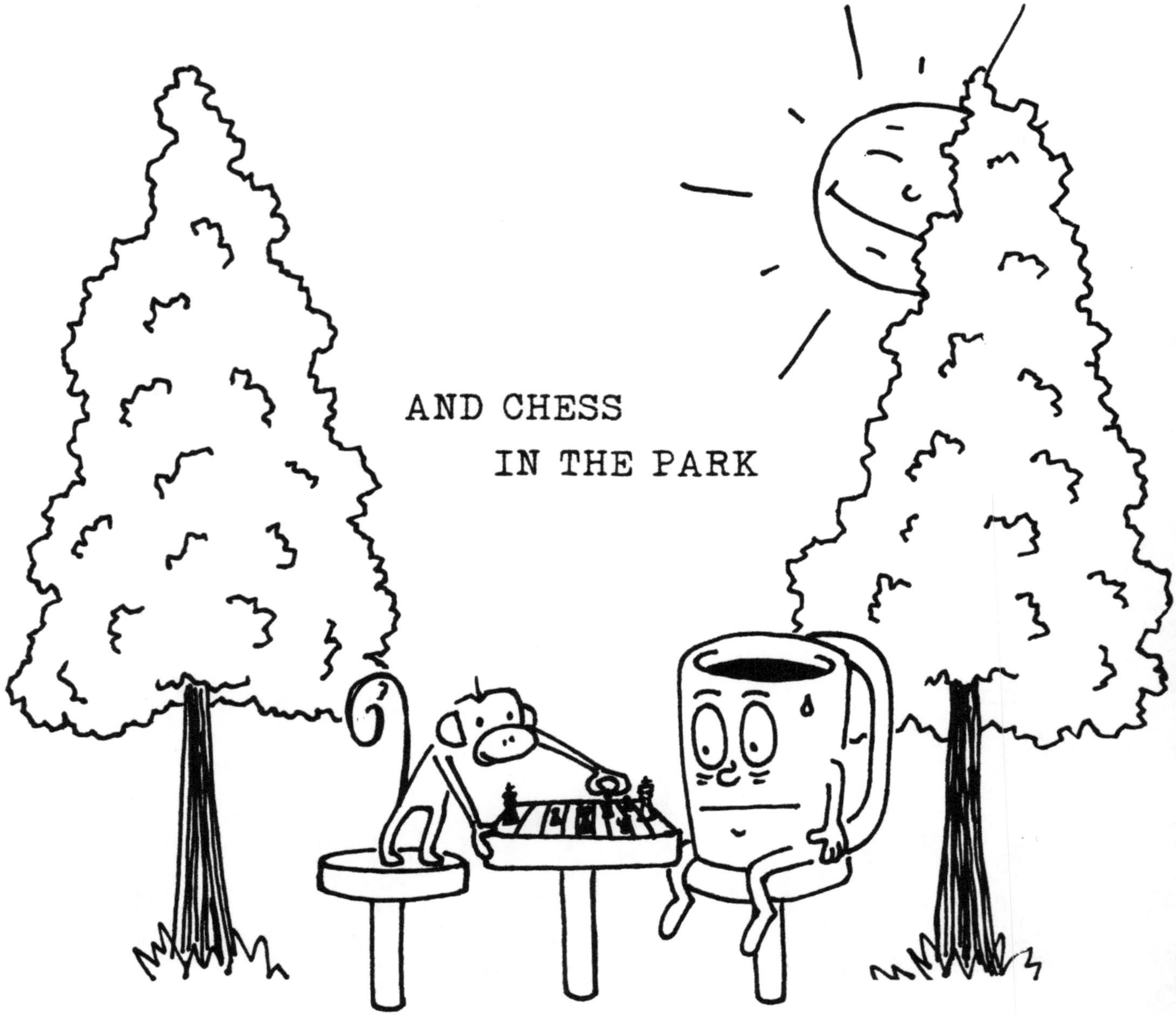
AND CHESS
IN THE PARK

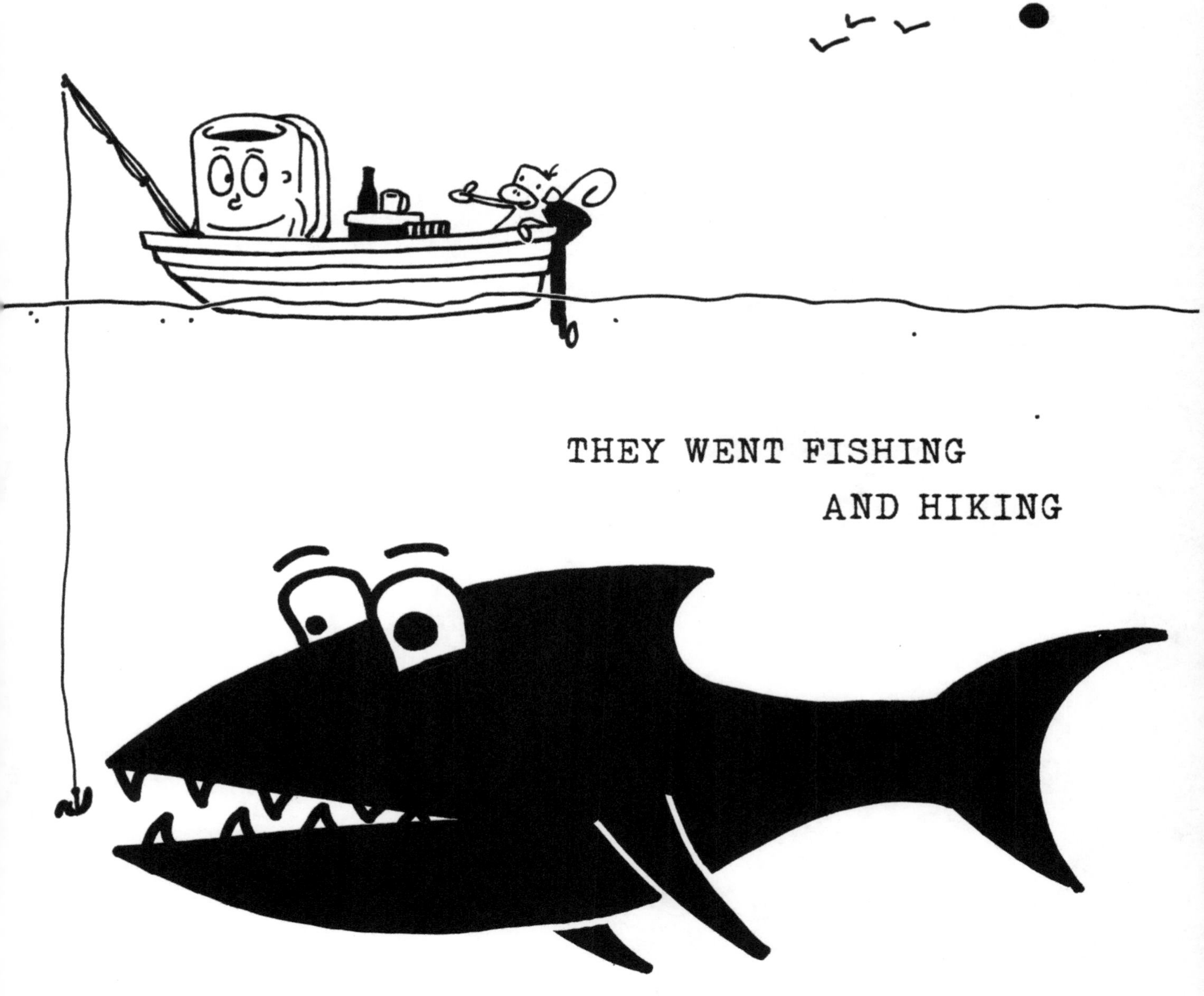

THEY WENT FISHING
AND HIKING

UNTIL IT
GOT DARK

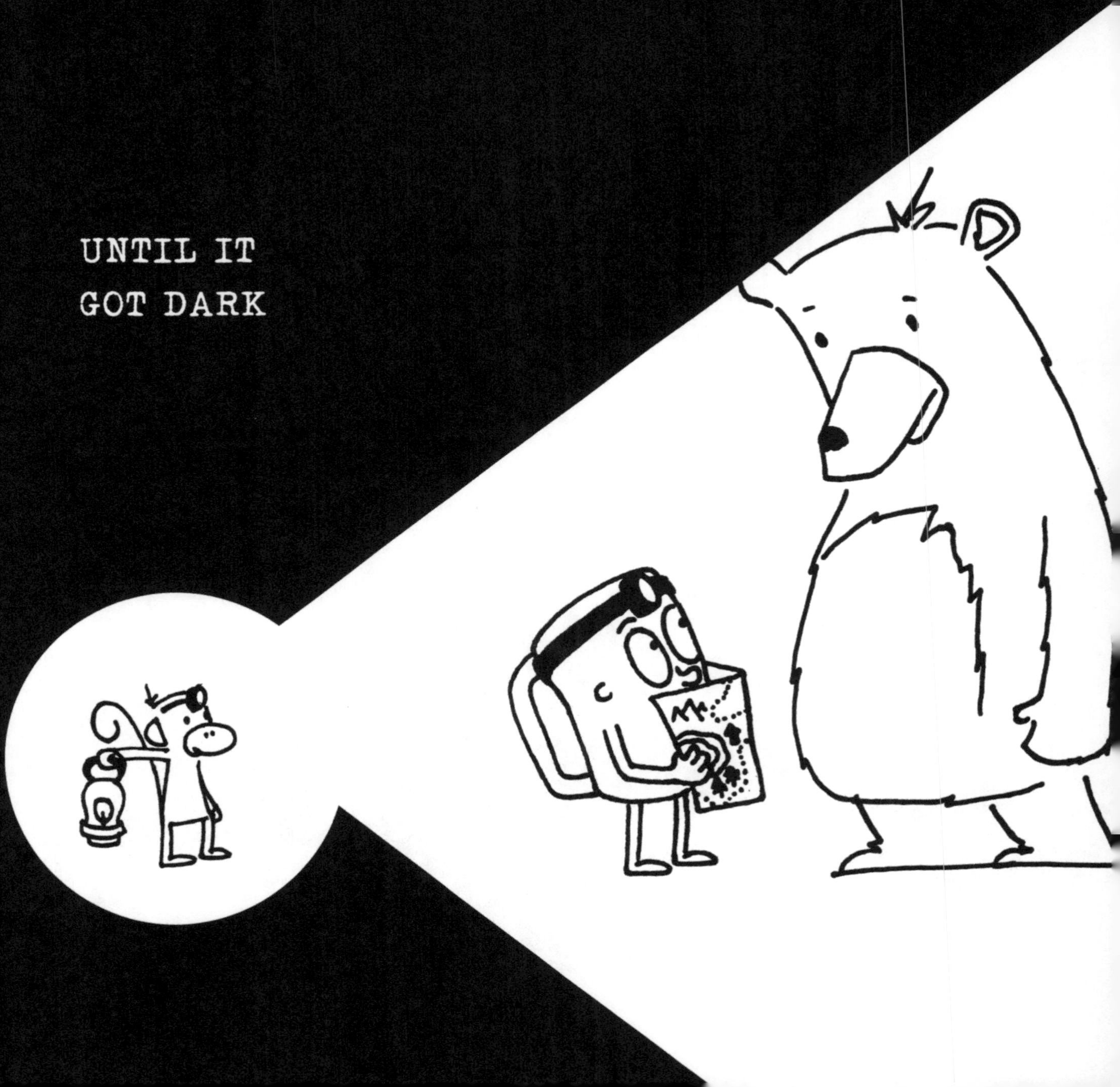

THEY BECAME BEST FRIENDS
(A PACT THEY'VE UPHELD)

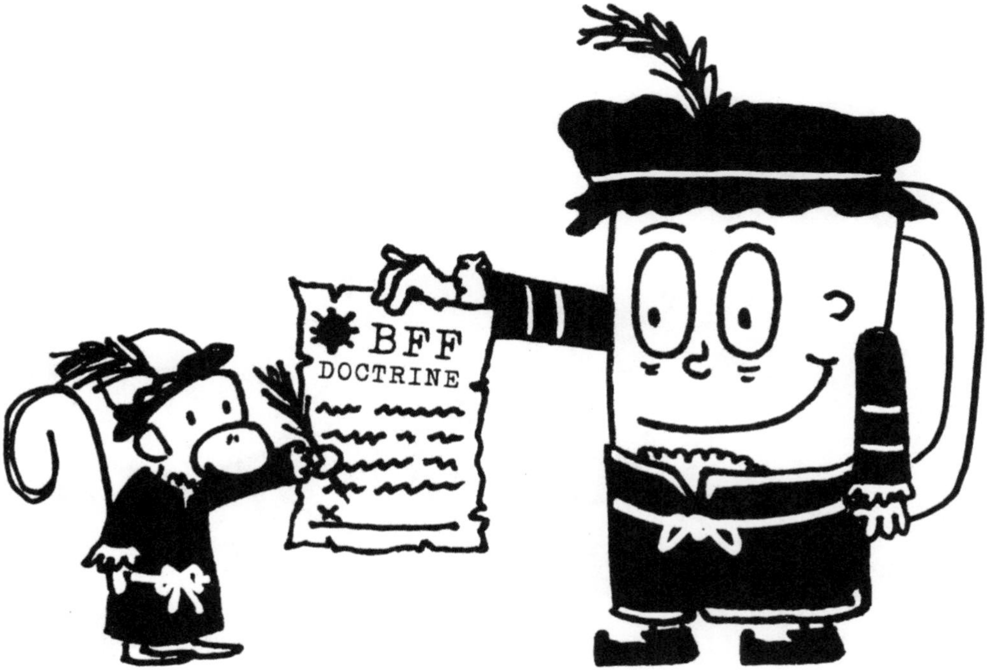
BFF
DOCTRINE

THEN THEY FROLICKED ON HOME

AND WATCHED RERUNS
OF "*SEINFELD*"...

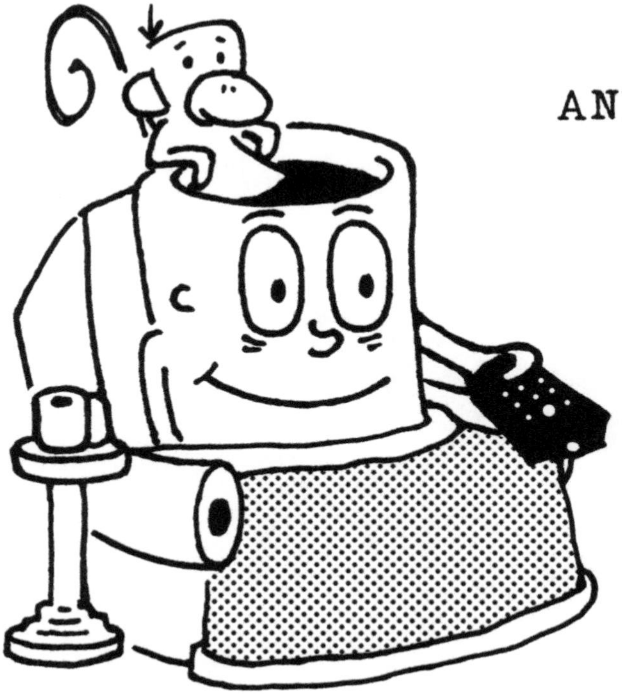

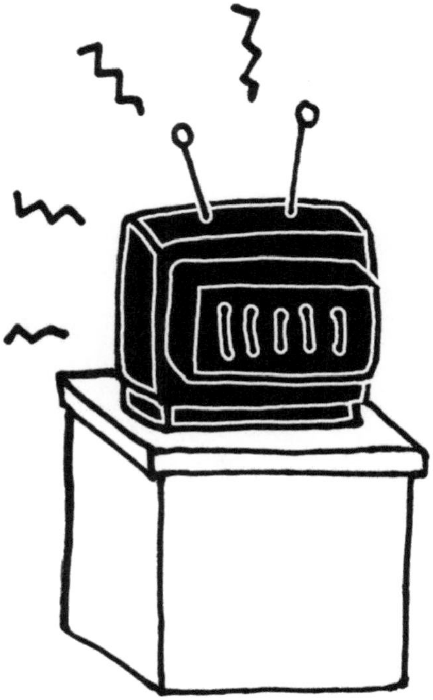

OSCAR AND JOE

THEY MAKE A GREA[illegible] TEAM

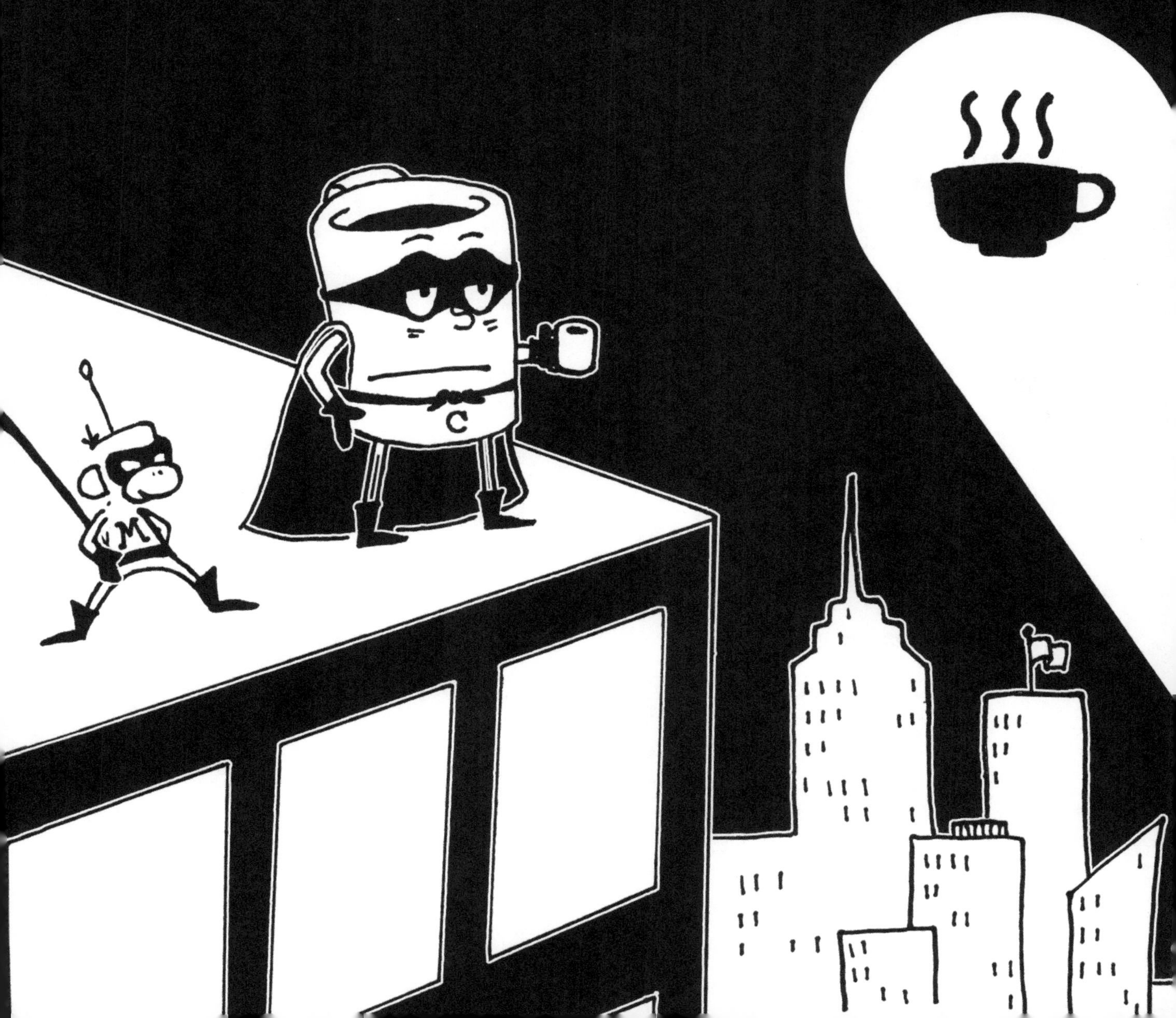

THEY'RE TRUE
COMPANIONS

OR THOUGH IT WOULD SEEM

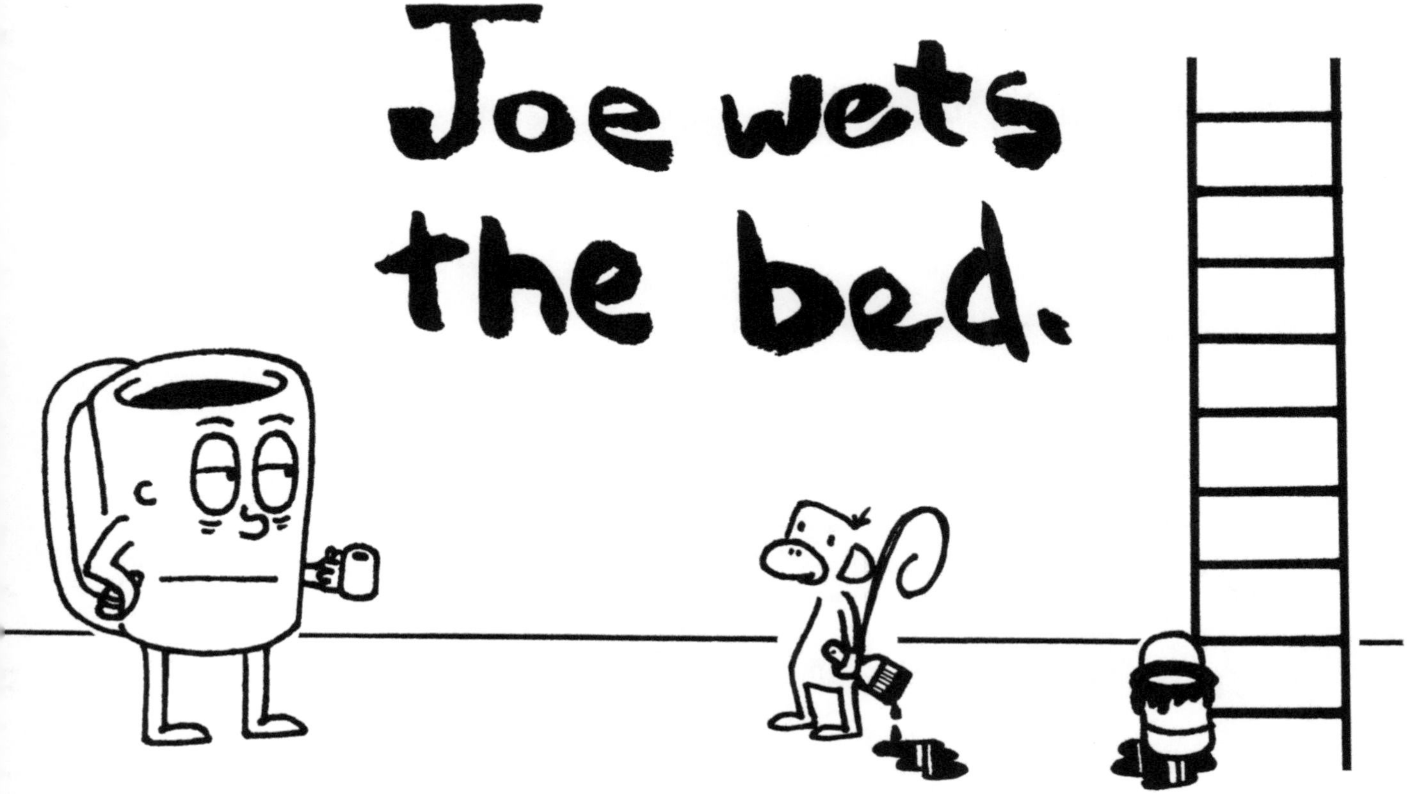
Joe wets the bed.

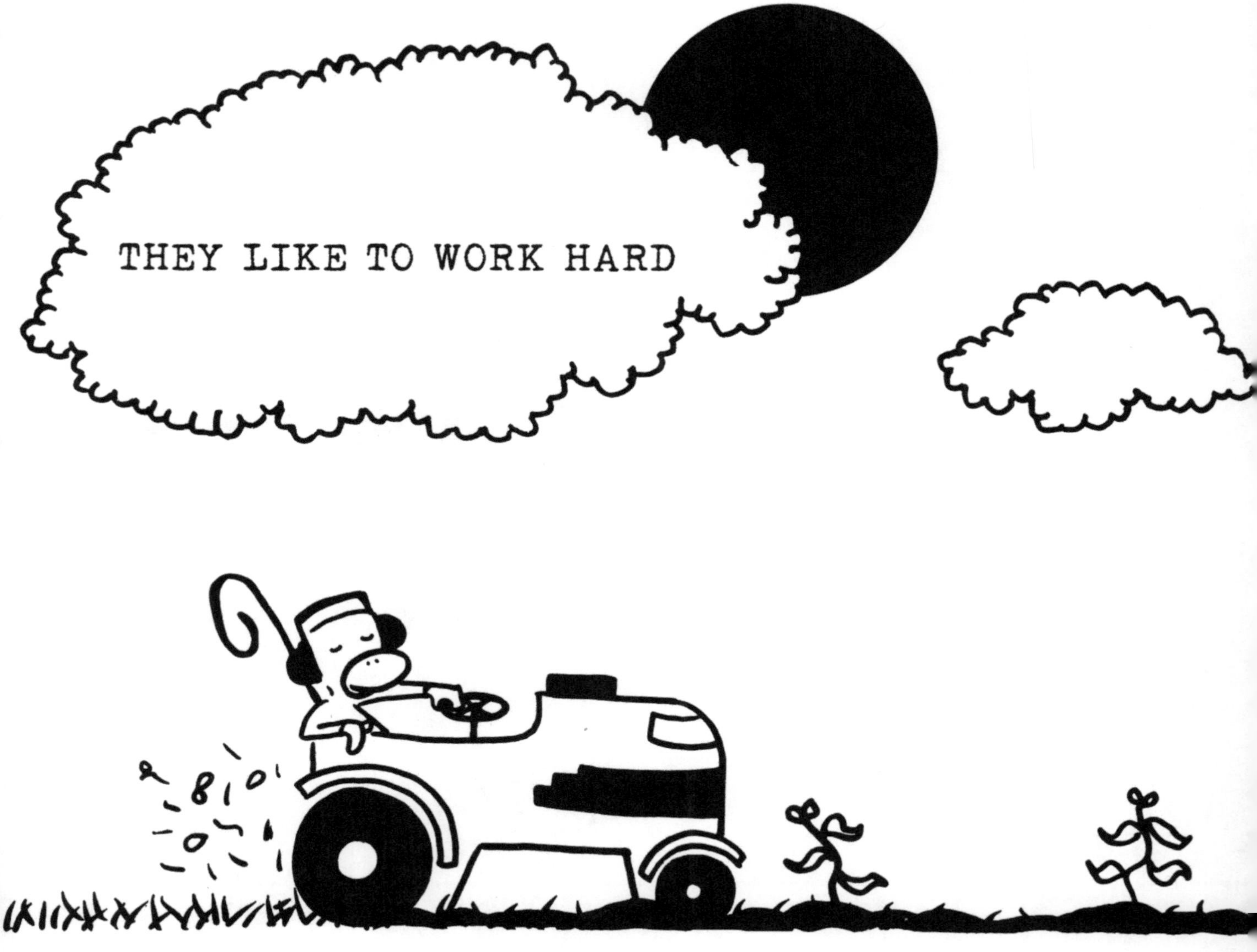
THEY LIKE TO WORK HARD

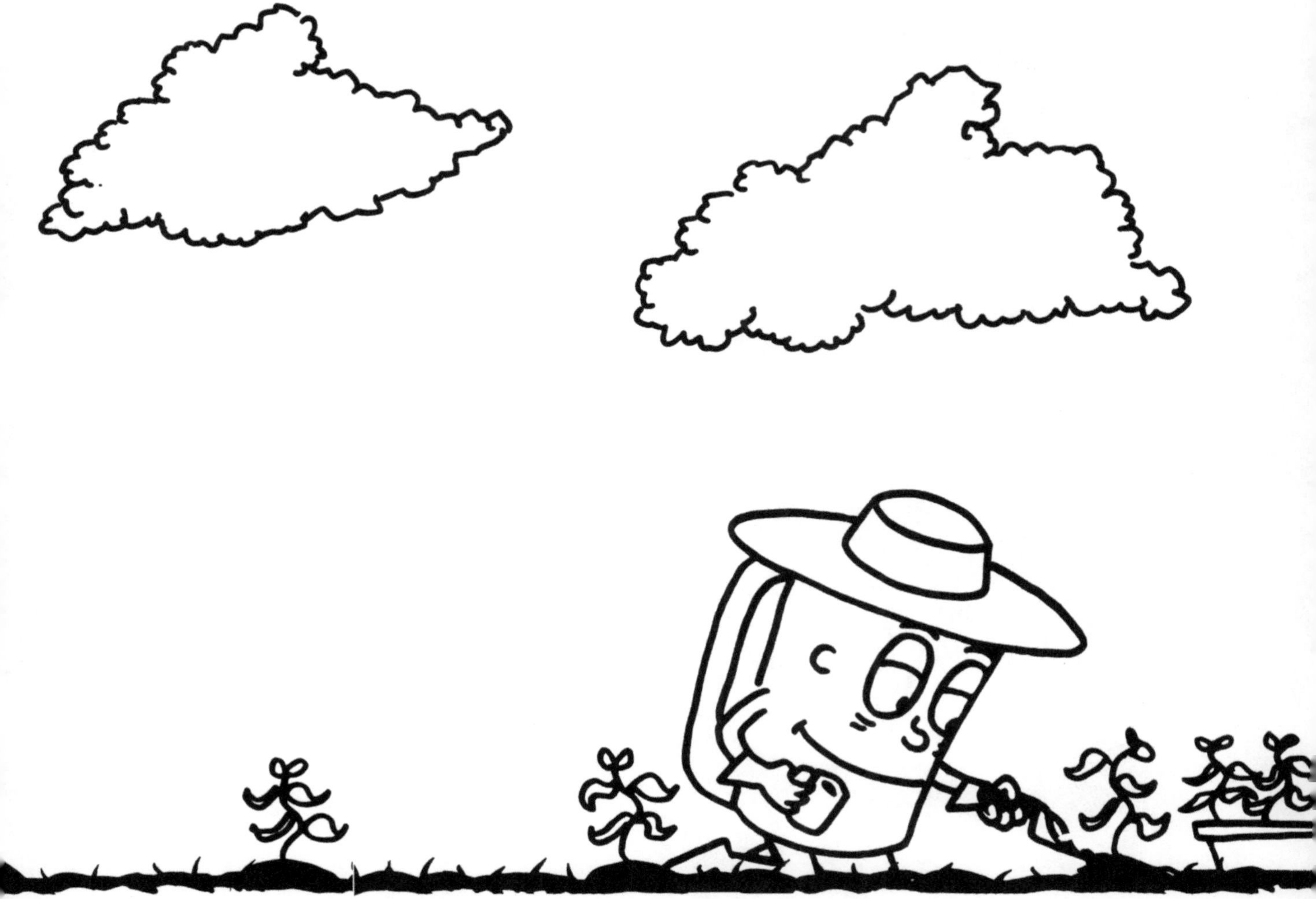

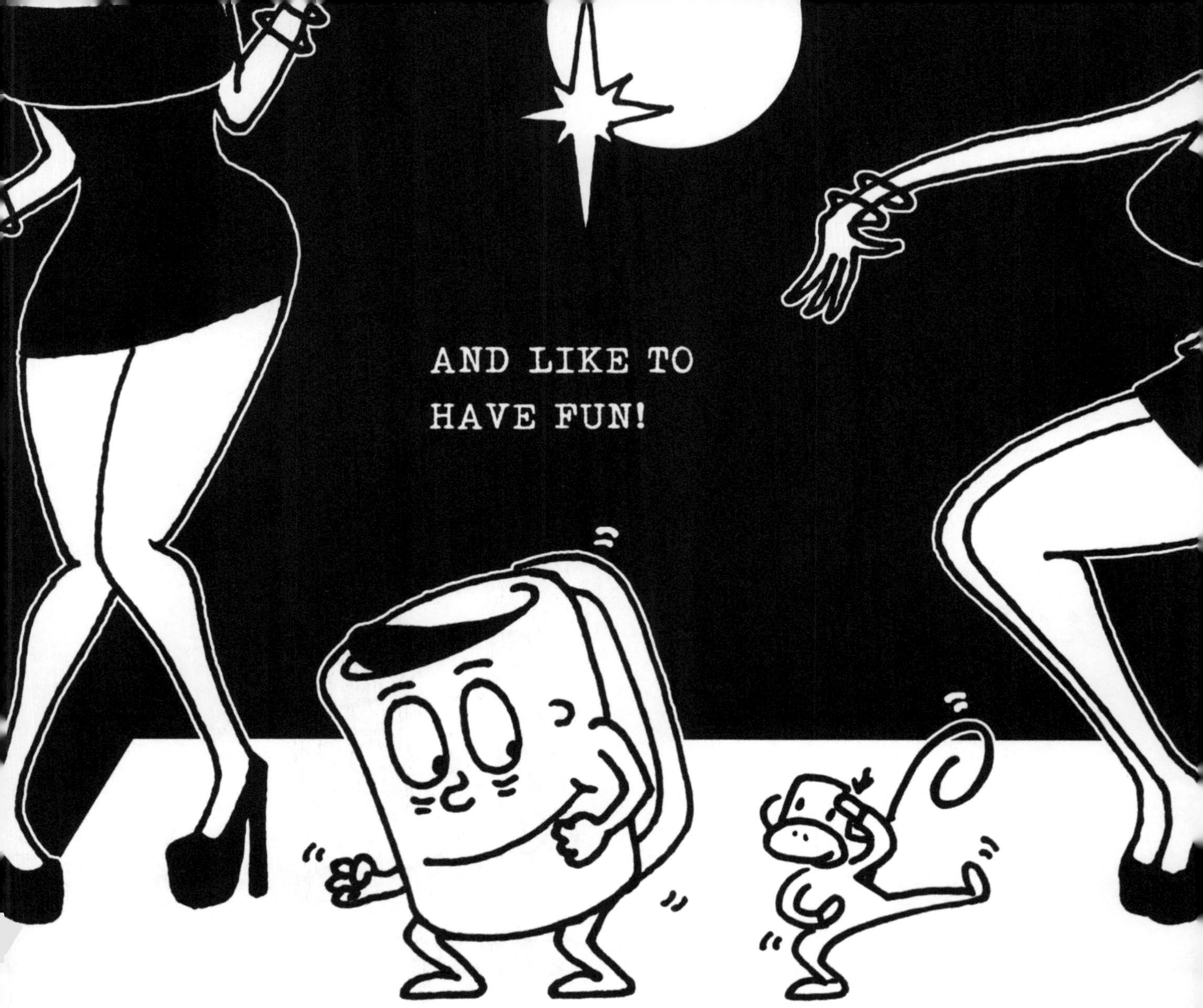
AND LIKE TO
HAVE FUN!

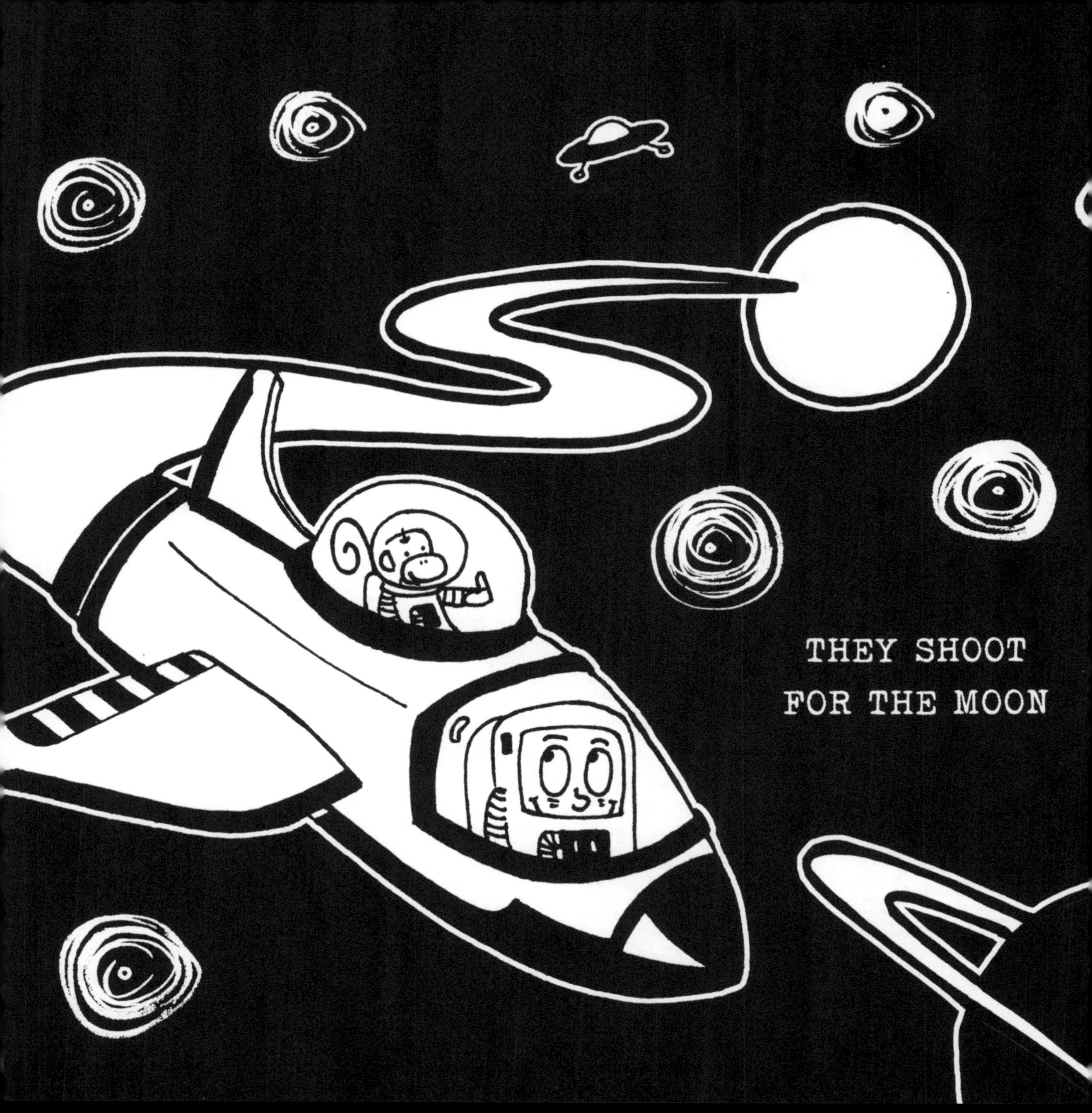
THEY SHOOT
FOR THE MOON

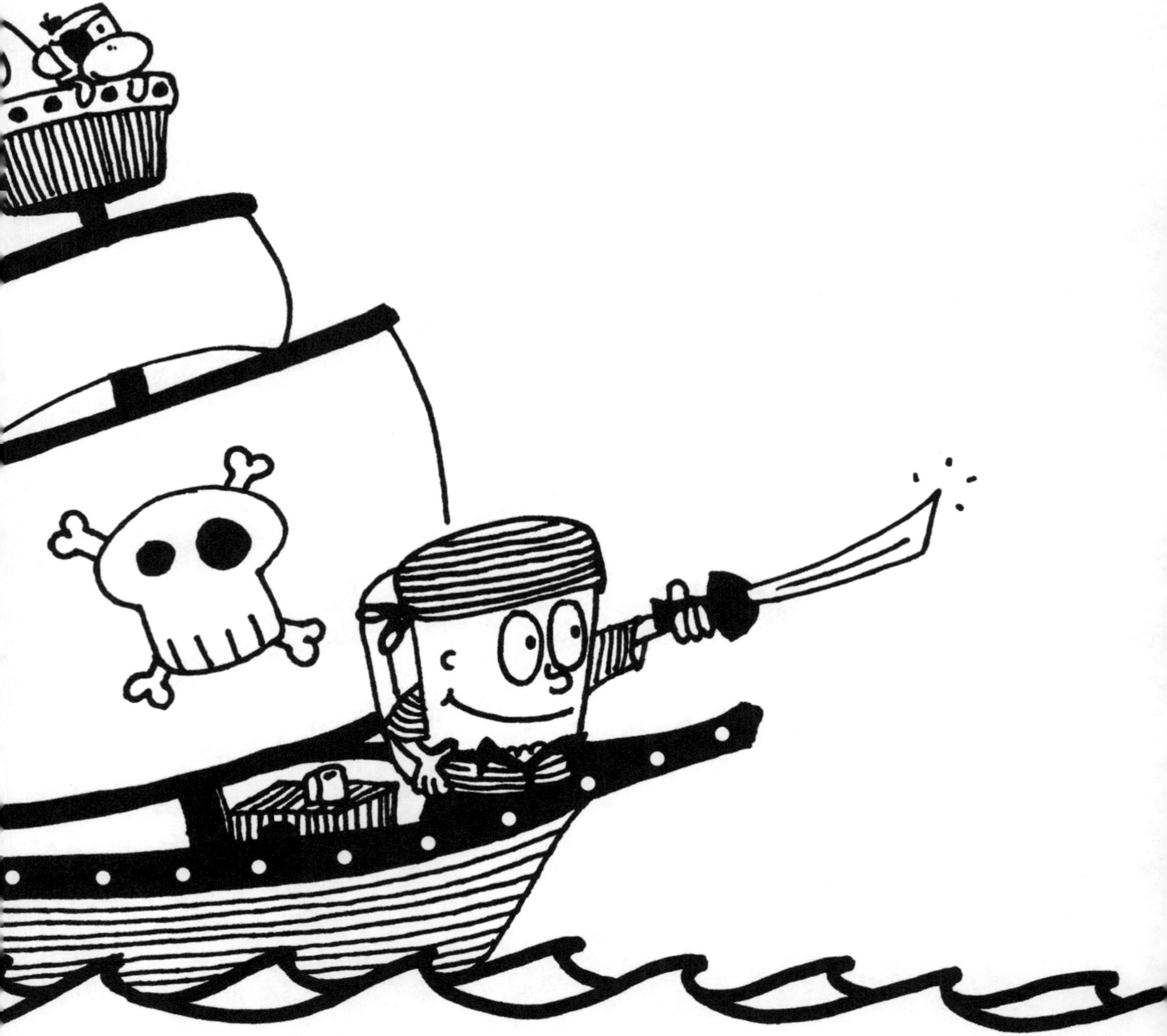

THEY SAIL TO THE SUN...

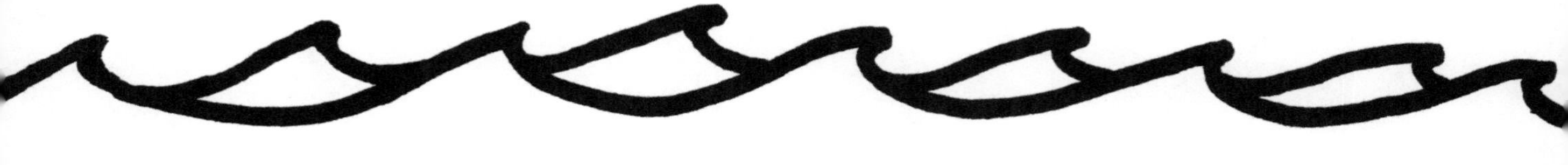

SO BE IN THE MOMENT

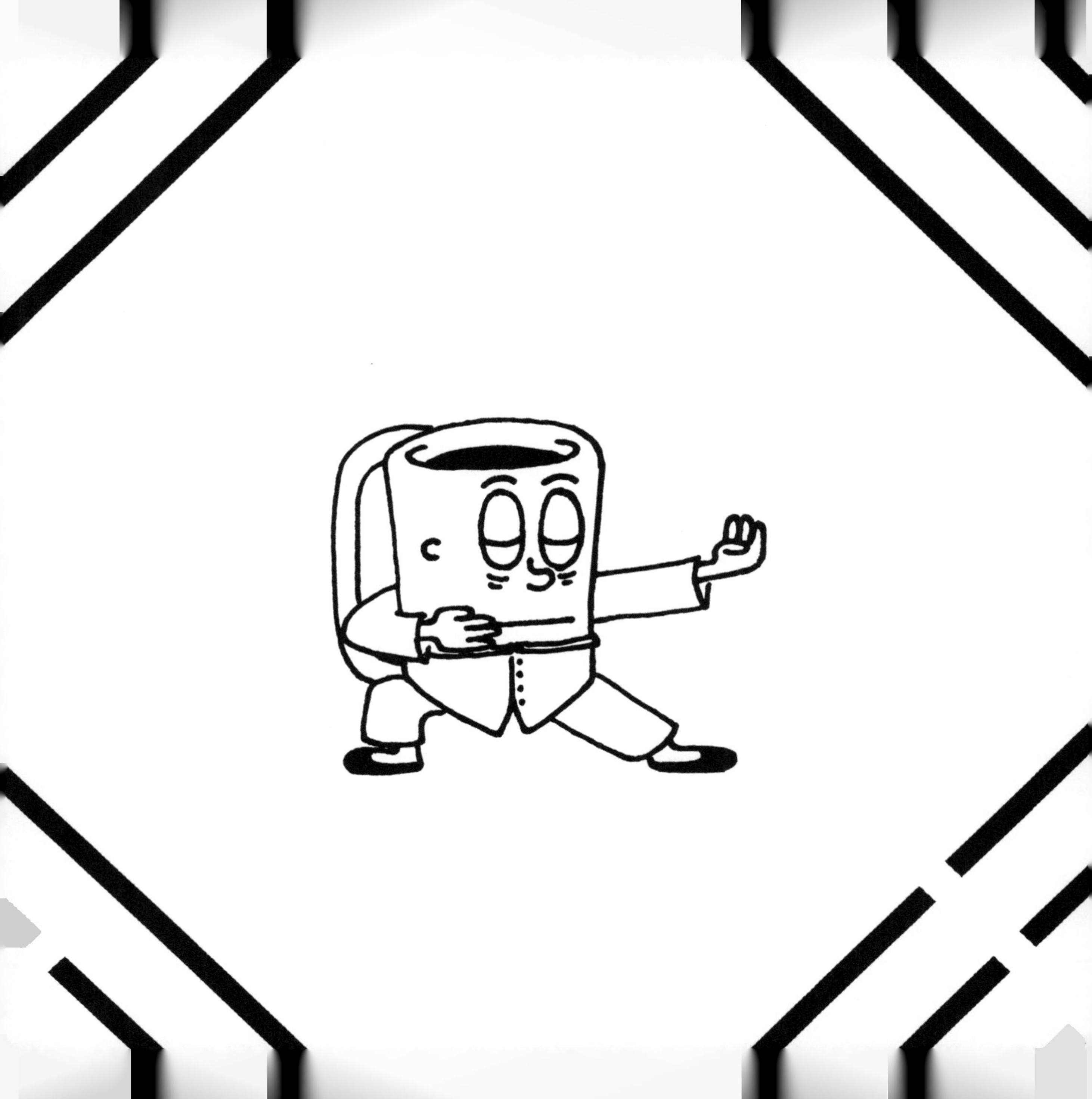

LEAVE THE PAST
IN ITS PLACE

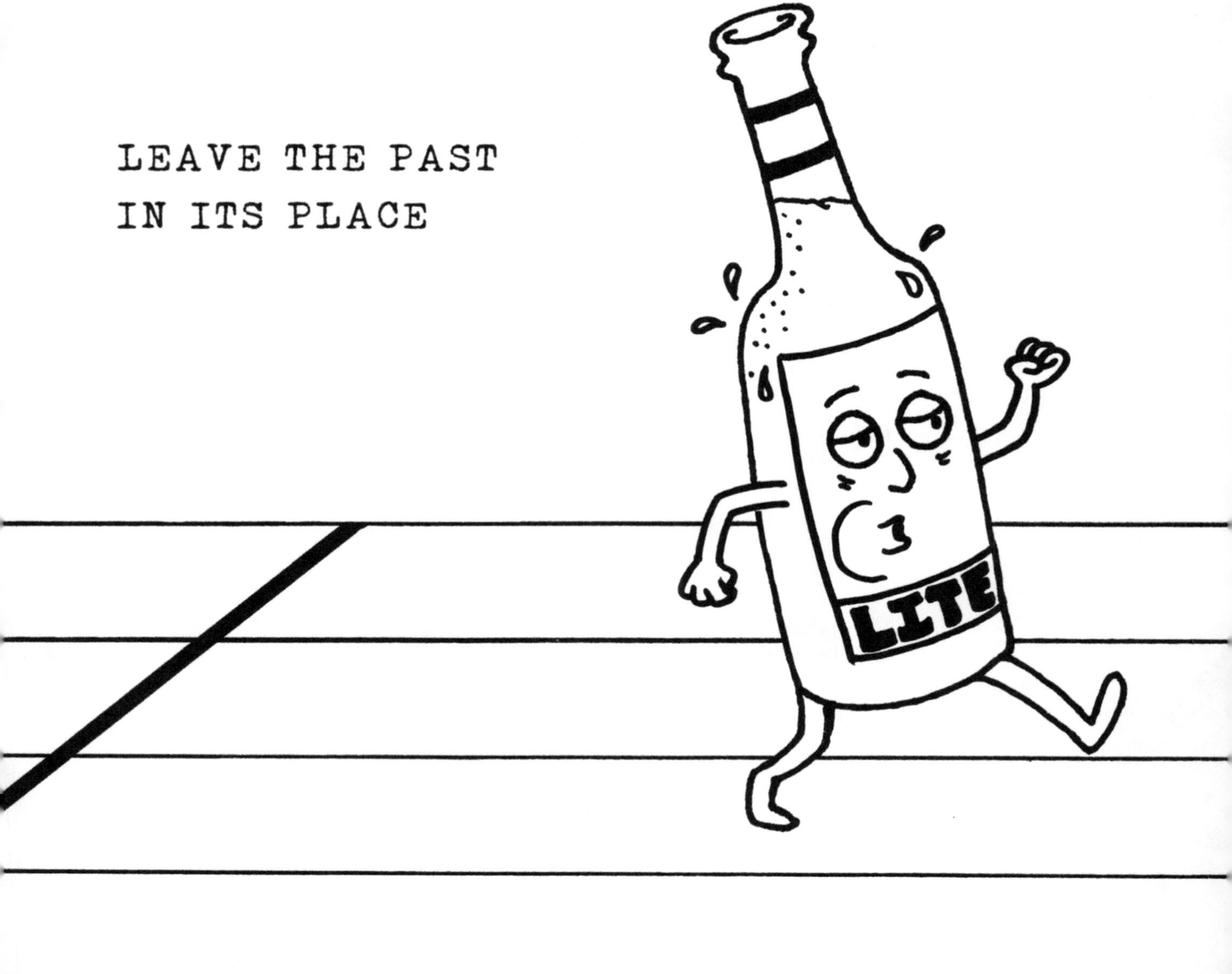
LITE

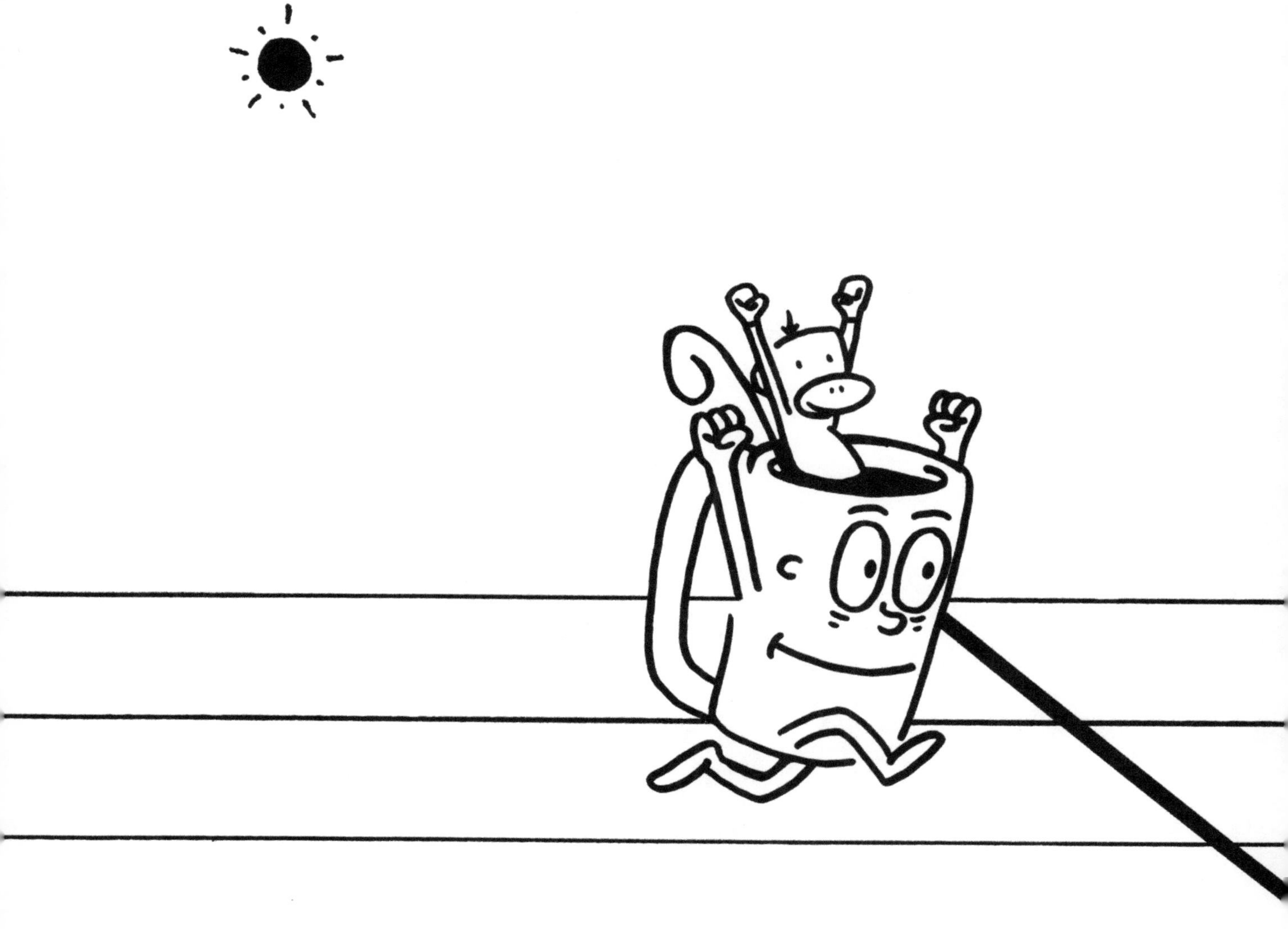

LIVE WITH A PURPOSE

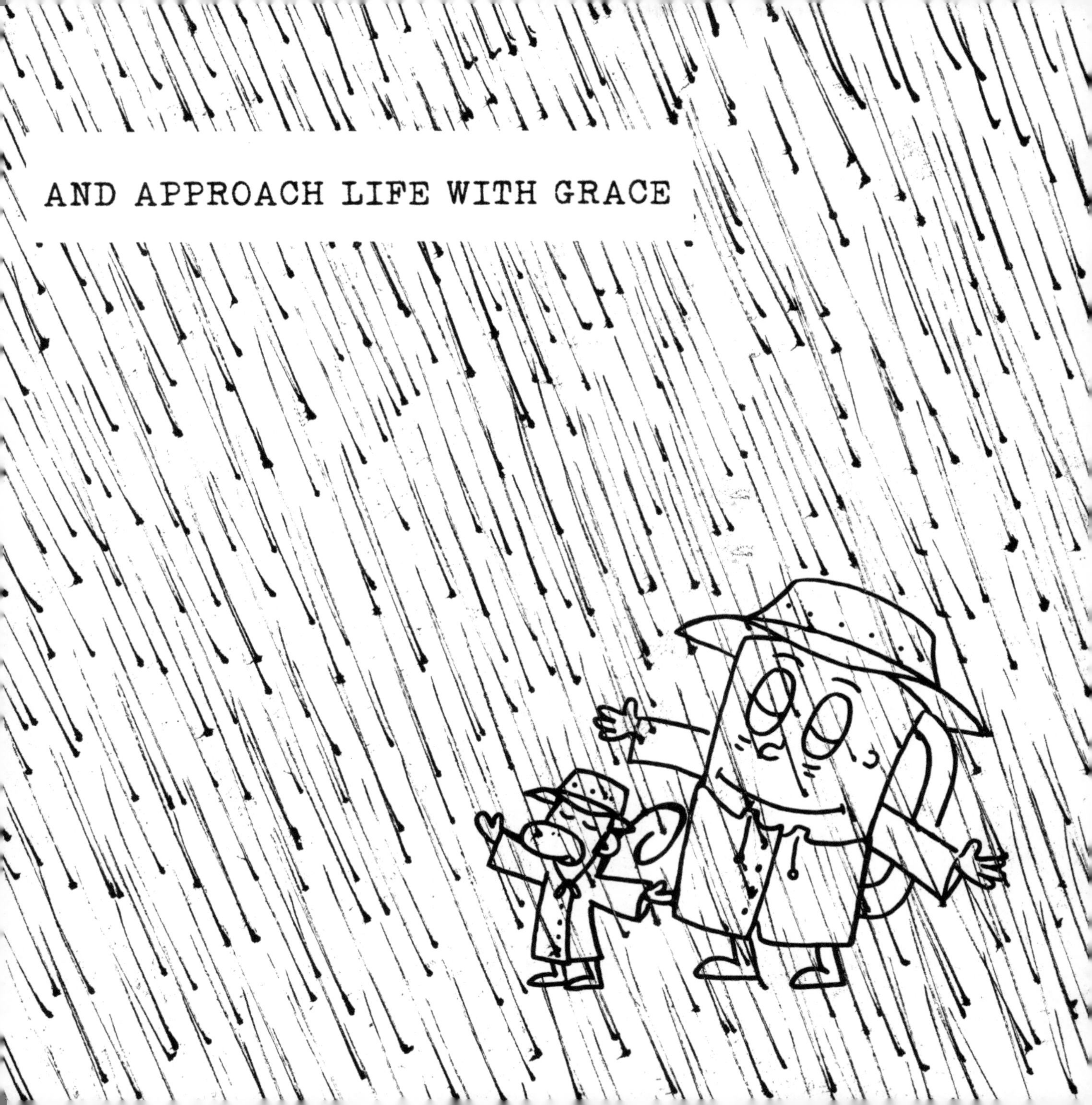
AND APPROACH LIFE WITH GRACE

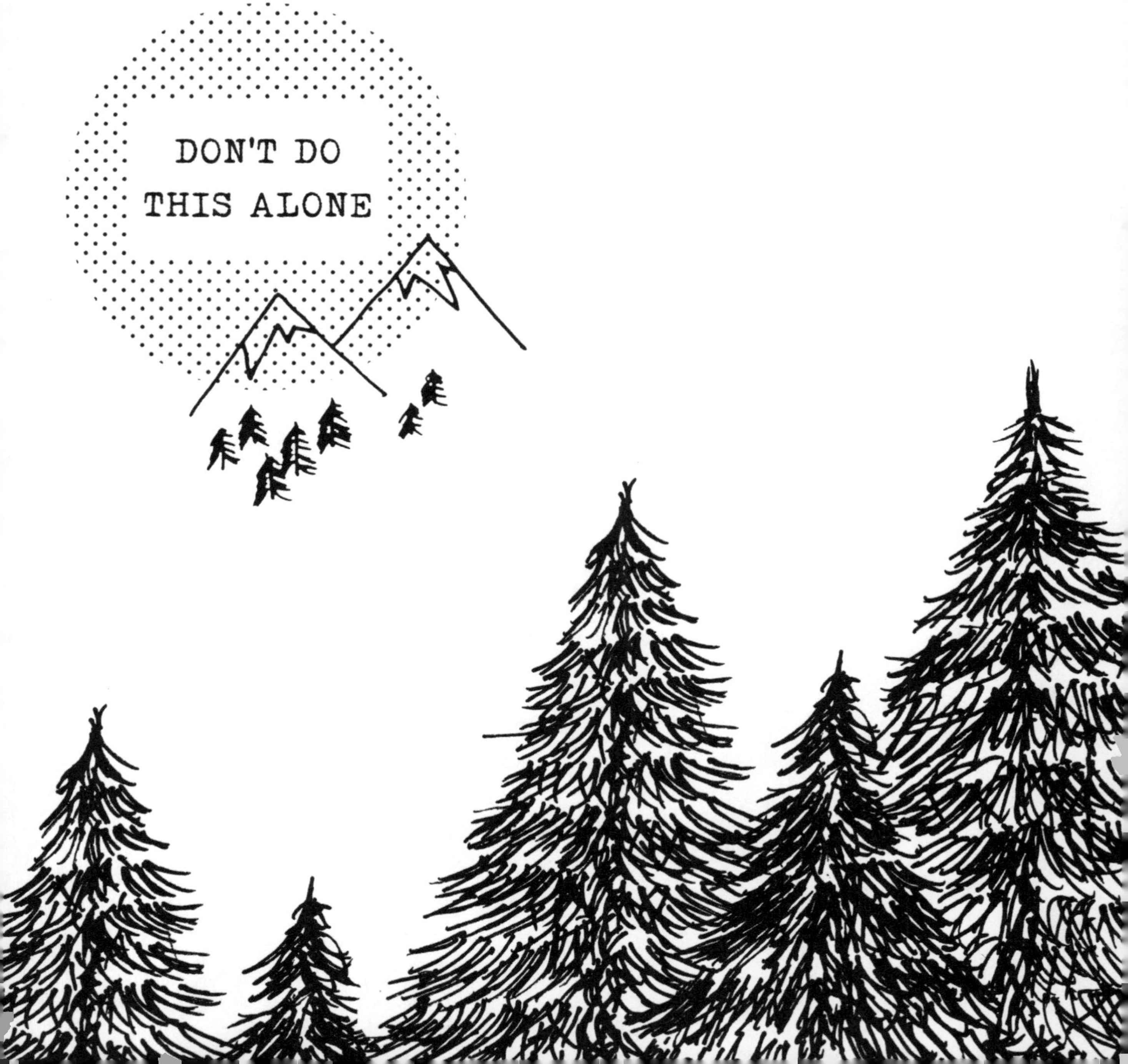
DON'T DO
THIS ALONE

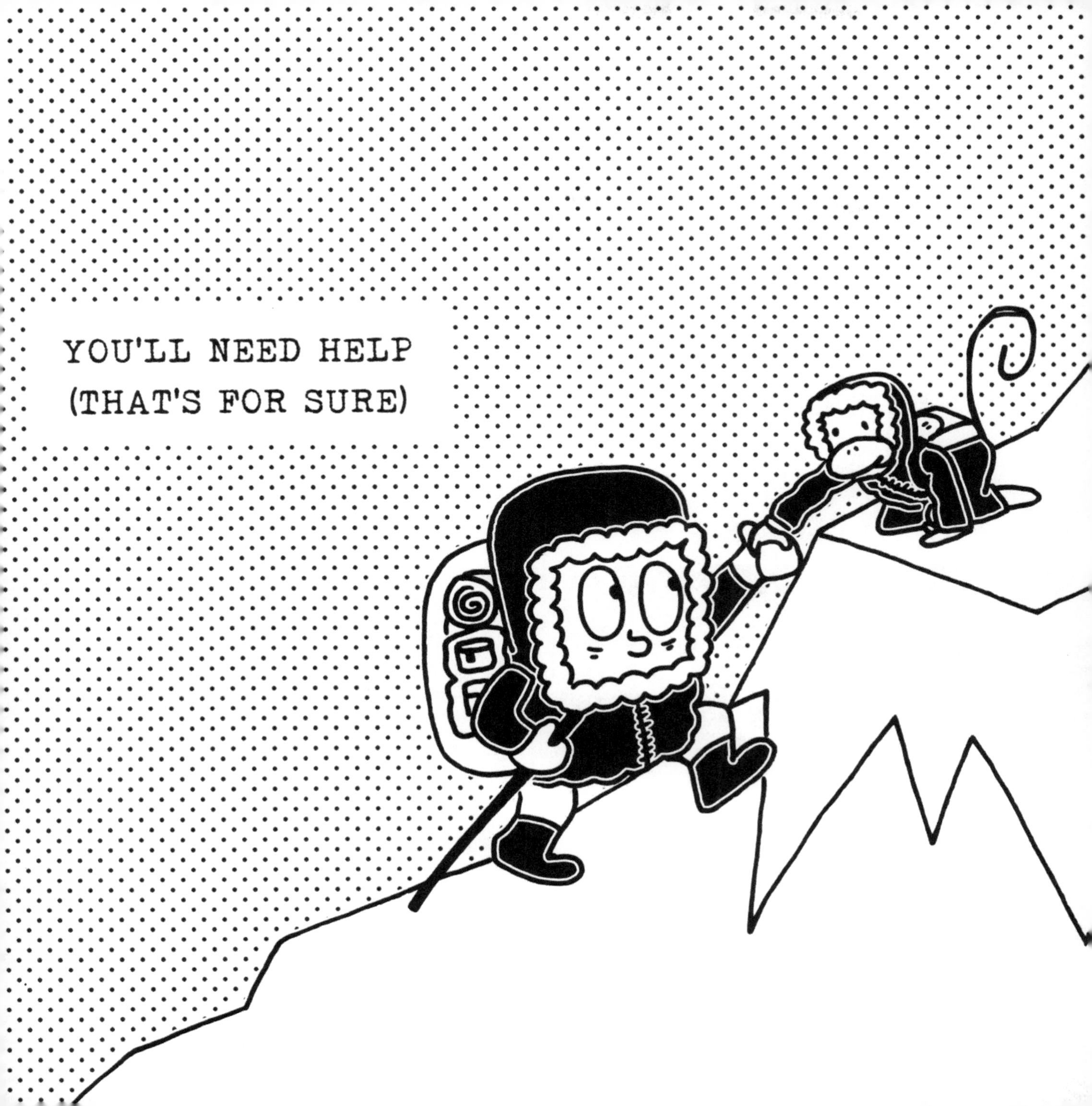
YOU'LL NEED HELP
(THAT'S FOR SURE)

SO KEEP YOUR
FRIENDS CLOSE

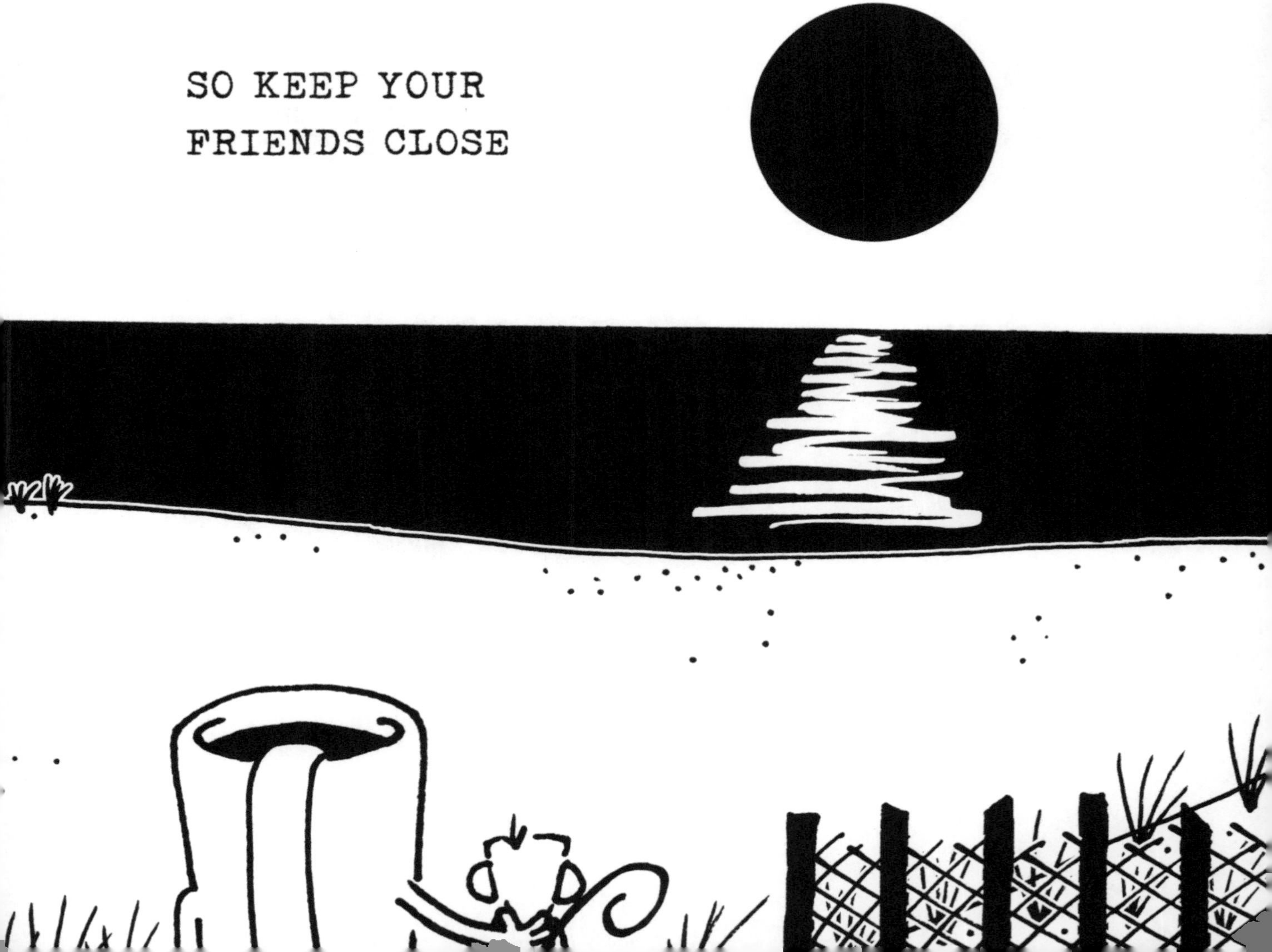

YOUR PEOPLE WHO CURE...

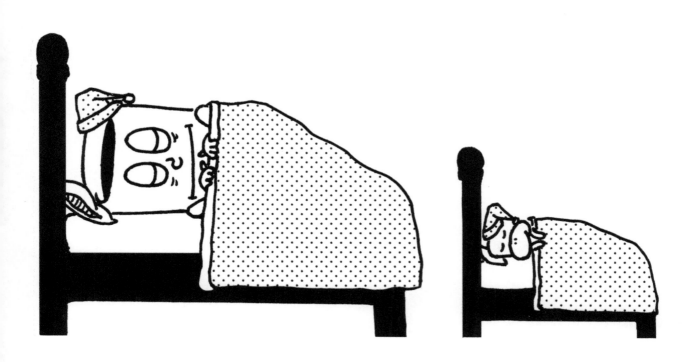

END🍞

CPSIA information can be obtained
at www.ICGtesting.com
Printed in the USA
LVHW021342031218
599056LV00032B/829/P